SWEATING BLOOD
MY LIFE IN SQUASH

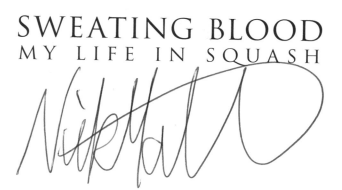

Nick Matthew is one of the greatest British squash
players of all time – a world No.1, world champion and
British Open champion. He is also a Commonwealth
Games gold medallist and the holder of a record number
of British national titles. He lives in Sheffield with his
wife Esme.

SWEATING BLOOD
MY LIFE IN SQUASH

BY WORLD CHAMPION
NICK MATTHEW

Published by internationalSPORTgroup 2013

Edited by: Dominic Bliss
Front and back cover photo: Moy Williams Photography
Typesetting and page layout: Nicola Thompson, Culver Design

Printed and bound by
Wyndeham Grange Limited

To my granddad, who is looking down on me, making
sure those drop shots go above the tin.

CONTENTS

FOREWORDS

Nick Matthew and I share a lot of similarities. The key ones are that we are both Sheffield born and bred, and, from an early age, we both found sport and got hooked on it – me on athletics, Nick on squash.

Our paths have frequently crossed, mainly during periods of training at the English Institute of Sport in Sheffield. We quickly became friends and admirers of each other's drive and ambition to be the best in the world at what we do.

Nick is one of the nicest and most humble people you could meet. But underneath all that he is one of the most driven and hard-working athletes I know. We have both had a long journey to the top of our sports and many hard knocks along the way – all part of the life of an elite athlete. What Nick has achieved in squash is nothing short of amazing. He has levels of fitness and agility that most sportspeople can only dream of, and has been number one in his sport globally. The media attention and sponsorship has not always been there for him but for most top athletes that is not the reason they do what they do. It is for the love of the sport.

I am sure when you read Nick's story you will see just how much he loves his sport and you'll realise the lengths he has gone to in order to become one of Britain's great sporting champions.

Jessica Ennis-Hill, Olympic heptathlon gold medallist

Nick Matthew is one of Britain's most extraordinary sportsmen. I first witnessed his combination of resilience and indefatigability in the Commonwealth Games in Melbourne when he came back from an impossible deficit against his long-time rival James Willstrop.

Nick was an inspiration in that match. I left the arena wondering about the high intensity of squash, its epic qualities. But more than anything I resolved to find out more about the athlete who had come out on top.

Over the years, I have watched Nick in action rather a lot. In everything he does, he embodies grit and determination. He is very nearly a running, lunging metaphor for the idea that if you dig deep enough, you can achieve anything. His willingness to push his body and mind further than his opponents is a revelation.

Squash is a tough sport. The financial rewards are rather trivial when compared with football and the like. But perhaps that lends it a particular charm and significance. It is played not for celebrity or riches but for motives that the Ancient Greeks would have recognised. That said, it is surely time for squash to come of age and for its stars to reap the rewards they have been long denied. It's cruel that athletes like Nick are not yet able to grace the Olympic stage. I hope one day squash will achieve the Olympic place it so richly deserves.

This book is a candid insight into the realities of squash, sometimes in painful detail. It chronicles the trivial and the profound. It is about squash but also about life. Nick pulls no punches. But, then, you would not expect him to.

Matthew Syed, journalist and Olympic table tennis player

DRAMATIS PERSONAE

Here are some of the wonderful characters you're going to meet in my book. Each has played a part – major or minor – in my life story.

Esme Matthew

I married my gorgeous Esme in the summer of 2013. She works for the English Institute of Sport in Manchester as a physiologist for the Great Britain Olympic cycling team. We first started dating in September 2010, just before the Commonwealth Games, so she was a massive influence on my winning two gold medals there. She has played the biggest role in my life ever since. I don't think it's too cheesy to say she is my best friend, my confidante and my soul mate.

My mum (Sue Matthew)

My mum is, on the exterior, the calmest, most composed person you could ever meet. On the interior, however, especially when I compete, she is a bag of nerves. She dotes on me just as you would expect the mother of an only child to do. Before she retired she was an English teacher at a secondary school in Rotherham, near my home town Sheffield.

My dad (Hedley Matthew)

My dad was my school PE teacher when I was a kid which means he cultivated both my interest in sport and my physical training while I was growing up. He was utterly selfless, ferrying me to countless tournaments when I was a junior player and investing his spare time and money in my development. He always pushed me hard without being a pushy parent. Eventually he retired from teaching to become manager of Hallamshire Tennis & Squash Club, my home club and the place I regularly train at. My dad now runs the shop at Hallamshire and watches more squash matches, both live and on Squash TV, than any other human being I know.

My granddad (Ronald Matthew)
My paternal granddad lived at home with us while I was growing up. He was one of my closest friends and nurtured in me a love of all sports. A former rugby player, he swears he would have been selected for the Wales national team if it hadn't been for World War II. He died in 2007 when I was away competing at the World Championships in Bermuda. Knowing my granddad, he probably waited until my match was over before he popped his clogs.

Auntie Sue (Suzanne Entwistle)
Auntie Sue is my dad's sister. A fiery redhead, she has taken on the role of head of the family in my granddad's absence. She is probably the member of my family to whom I am closest, perhaps because she shares my characteristics (she is a Leo like me), especially when it comes to stubbornness and determination. A former nurse, she lives in Skipton, in North Yorkshire, with her husband Brian.

DP (my coach, David Pearson)
My coach and mentor, DP has one of the greatest tactical and technical minds in modern squash. As a player he competed for England and reached top 20 in the world but it's as a coach that he has really excelled. He was the England national coach for 15 years and, as well as advising me, he guided both Peter Nicol and Cassie Jackman to world titles and world No.1 rankings.

Neil Guirey (my best friend)
Neil is my best friend and someone I can trust as if my life depends on it. I first met him on the squash court when I was just nine years old and we played together for Yorkshire juniors at all ages until our late teens. Nowadays he is the head professional at the famous Abbeydale Park Rackets & Fitness Club in Sheffield and acts as my secondary coach when DP's not around. I love having him at tournaments because, while I tend to be the storm, he is always the calm.

Mark Campbell (my trainer)
A Kiwi with a background working in rugby, Mark has been my physical trainer since 2007, the man who oversees the fitness side

of my squash. Known affectionately as Cones, due to the shape of his head, he formulated the legendary Rumble fitness circuits which helped transform me into one of the fittest men in squash. Mark works as lead strength and conditioning coach for the English Institute of Sport in Sheffield. When he's not killing me in the gym he's one of the few people I know who plays more squash than I do.

Mark Bawden (my sports psychologist)
Head psychologist for the English Institute of Sport and the England cricket team, Mark is the man who keeps my brain in order. Without him I would be a mental case.

Jade Elias (England squash physio)
Head physio for England Squash and based at the English Institute of Sport in Manchester, Jade ensures I don't fall apart after tough training sessions and even harder matches. Without her I never could have competed this long on the tour. She also takes credit for originally setting me up with my wife.

Paul Walters (my manager)
You might call Paul Walters Mr Squash. As well as being my manager – and the man responsible for all my sponsorship and business deals – he has been director of multiple British and World Opens, and heads up sports marketing company internationalSPORTgroup. Paul is one of my closest friends and the most supportive manager any athlete could wish for. He deserves massive credit for being my verbal punchbag over the years.

Rob Johnson (my Sheffield physio)
Head physio at the English Institute of Sport in Sheffield, and an ex-professional footballer for Luton Town, Rob has been my physio since I was 21. When I was younger he saved my career by curing my back problems.

Derry Suter (my massage therapist)
Derry, or Magic Hands, as we refer to him, is the self-proclaimed "best soft-tissue therapist in the world". I'm inclined to believe him. He keeps me in one piece when I'm back from tour and he knows my

body better than anyone else on the planet, my wife included. Derry treats many world-class athletes from the English Institute of Sport in Sheffield, including Olympic gold medallist Jessica Ennis-Hill.

Mark Hornby (my ex-coach)
Mark led me through my early – and most formative – years in squash, coaching me from the age of 10 to 19. He taught me all the fundamentals you see in my game today, including my formidable volley and my strong mental game.

FORMER PLAYERS

Jahangir Khan (The Conqueror)
Who could possibly deny this man the accolade of being the greatest squash player of all time? As well as his six World Opens, and 10 British Opens, the Pakistani player holds the honour of being unbeaten in competitive play between the years of 1981 and 1986: a total of 555 straight match victories. It was astounding. Guinness World Records honours this as the longest winning streak from any athlete in any top professional sport. No wonder Jahangir is nowadays treated like royalty.

Jansher Khan (King Khan)
With the same nationality and surname as Jahangir (although not a direct relative), Jansher was the man who finally, in the late 1980s, broke Jahangir's stranglehold on the sport, eventually winning eight World Opens (a record) and six British Opens. In my opinion, he's the second greatest squash player of all time.

Jonah Barrington (The Black Baron)
The godfather of British squash, Jonah is responsible for transforming the sport in this country from its amateurish status to a culture of pure professionalism. He is universally recognised as one of the fittest athletes the world has ever seen. It's thanks to Jonah that squash became so prominent in the 1970s and 1980s.

Peter Nicol (The Boss)

Peter will probably be most remembered in sports history for famously switching allegiance from Scotland to England halfway through his career. But we should never forget the amazing achievements of this now retired left-hander. For five straight years he held the world No.1 spot – the first Briton ever to do so. He also won one World Open, two British Opens and four Commonwealth Games gold medals. It was Peter who, in the 1990s, brought to an end the reign of the mighty Jansher Khan. Not surprisingly, he was a massive role model for me in my early days, someone I learned more from than any other player. I believe he's one of the greatest British athletes of all time. If my life depended on winning a squash match, I would choose Peter to play it.

Jonathon Power (The Magician)

This Canadian maverick was Peter Nicol's arch rival for most of his career and he couldn't have been more different in character. Thanks to his emotional outbursts and verbal exchanges with referees – not to mention the headbands and scraggly hair – he was often considered the John McEnroe of squash. He had an astounding skill, using stunning shots and deception to demolish opponents, reach the world No.1 position and win the World Open, the British Open and singles medals at two different Commonwealth Games.

David Palmer (The Marine)

Imagine a typical, no-nonsense Aussie sportsman and you'll have a pretty accurate picture of David Palmer: 6ft 3ins, built like a brick wall, never took prisoners, always played like the ultimate professional. A former world No.1, he won a staggering two World Opens, four British Opens and a Commonwealth Games silver medal. He is one of the best pressure players of all time, with some deciding-game comebacks that can only be described as legendary.

Thierry Lincou (Le Patron)

Hailing from Reunion Island, one of France's overseas departments, Thierry was the first Frenchman ever to reach world No.1 and win the World Open. One of the fittest players and best lateral movers ever in squash, he used to scuttle like a crab across the middle of the court, always controlling the T and often proving impossible to break down. Despite being renowned for his incredibly slow starts to matches, once he had you in his sights he was like a missile honing in on its target.

CURRENT PLAYERS

James Willstrop (The Marksman)
Hailing from Pontefract Squash & Leisure Club in West Yorkshire, James has been a colleague and peer since our junior days. But we were never close friends. Our relationship became permanently strained after a tempestuous British Open final in 2009. James has a marksman's touch, accuracy and control, plus an enviable reach thanks to his 6ft 4in frame. He's also, in my opinion, one of the toughest, never-say-die competitors I've ever played. Hence his former world No.1 ranking and two Commonwealth Games silver medals.

Ramy Ashour (The Artist)
This man holds the racket as if he is painting beautiful strokes with a paintbrush. But don't be fooled – he can be lethal and is perhaps one of the most outrageous shotmakers the game of squash has ever seen. He has a totally unique style, with barely a single textbook shot in his armoury. Bubbly in personality and a great crowd favourite, he also has a very complex character and has admitted on numerous occasions to being less than sane. Twice World Champion before his 26th birthday, he has the potential to dominate the sport in the years to come.

Gregory Gaultier (Asterix)
On court this emotional Frenchman always wears his heart on his sleeve. He plays incredibly fast and powerfully but is often extremely volatile, although he seems to have matured since becoming a father. Along with James Willstrop, Ramy Ashour and me, he has been vying for the world top spot over the last couple of years, reaching it once so far. He has won a British Open and has been runner-up in three World Open finals.

Amr Shabana (The Maestro)

Amr's nickname really sums him up. If you wrote a squash coaching textbook, this would be the player you would feature. Throughout his career he has grown from being a rebel, tearaway kid to four-times world champion and world No.1 for three and a half years straight. Of all the current players he is perhaps the most graceful and sportsmanlike.

Karim Darwish (The Dark Prince)

He may have reached the world No.1 spot in 2009, and he may have been runner-up at the World Open, yet Karim has never really achieved the same recognition as his fellow Egyptians Ramy Ashour or Amr Shabana. That might be because he's a very private guy. Nevertheless, he has the best front forehand I've ever played against. And he's deadly with a trickle boast.

Peter Barker (The Metronome)

One of my best friends on the tour, Londoner Peter Barker is an exceptionally consistent player who has been as high as No.5 in the world. He's great fun to hang out with, and is one of my regular hotel roommates on the tour. I'd say he's probably the only person I've met who's more brutally honest than I am.

Alister Walker (The Predator)

This Botswanan player who used to compete for England was my main training partner for five years. With his dreadlocks and funky clothes, he is generally considered the player with the best on-court fashion sense on the PSA tour. (Not that that's difficult.) He now lives in the USA.

Adrian Grant

Adrian is another regular roommate of mine on the tour. We have had a lot of fun together, especially in our younger days when we were partners in crime, often getting into a few scrapes. Born in London, he lived in Halifax for a number of years and became a regular training partner of mine before recently moving back home. Adrian has been as high as No.9 in the world. In 2010 we teamed up to win the gold medal in the Commonwealth Games men's doubles.

CHAPTER 1

My precious squash hands

In which Nick has a playground scrap, introduces us to
his family (including his legendary granddad) and gets
invited on the panel of A Question of Sport.

October 1993 and I'm rolling around in the playground fighting
another schoolkid, Jonathan Caterer. Despite the fact that neither of
us has yet managed to throw a proper punch, my jacket sleeves are
pulled up over my fists so I don't risk damaging my precious squash
hands. For the group of kids huddled round us, cheering us on, it's a
pretty pathetic sight. I've got Jonathan in a headlock and we're both
writhing around in the mud. To this day, it's still the only fight I've
ever had.

It all started courtesy of my old man, Hedley. He was the PE
teacher at my secondary school, High Storrs, and the previous day
he'd handed out a detention to Jonathan Caterer. Rightly miffed,
Jonathan was now taking it out on the teacher's son. Knowing me,
I'd probably gloated over his misfortune and deserved a bit of a
slapping. Just as long as my squash hands were protected.

It's not easy having your dad working as a teacher at your school.
You become defined by it. More often than not I was referred to as
"Mr Matthew's son". Fortunately my dad was a PE teacher so most
kids enjoyed his lessons. God help me if his subject had been maths
or chemistry.

Nevertheless, I got a fair bit of stick. He could be quite strict
when he needed to be, hence Caterer's detention. Turn up for PE
without your sports kit and, yes, you would be doing it in your
underpants. Fail to put in the effort on a cross-country run and
you'd definitely be in for some press-ups as punishment. It's normal,

I suppose, for maligned kids to take out their grievances on the teacher's son. I'd probably have done the same.

So imagine what the other kids thought of me when my dad appointed me captain of both my school year's cricket and football teams. Accusations of nepotism were flying around the pitch like errant shots on goal. Actually, when it came to the cricket, I probably was the best man for the job... even if I say so myself. I was a decent all-rounder and at one stage I had batting trials for Sheffield boys. Thanks to my squash training and endless hours of watching sport on TV, I had a very analytical sports brain, and I was good at working out batting and bowling orders, and setting the fields. But as skipper of football there was definitely a bit of nepotism going on. I was a good central midfielder, a good workhorse, and I ran my socks off, but there were kids in the second 11 who were more skilful than me. And they were constantly reminding me of this fact. As a result I had to prove myself, justify my position as captain and demonstrate that what I lacked in skill I possessed in leadership.

It seemed to work since I ended up captaining our school all the way to Sheffield champions in my first two years at secondary school. Maybe my dad had been testing me. Maybe he knew that if he promoted me above my station it would teach me to work hard at excelling in sport. I always knew deep down, however, that neither cricket nor football were the right sports for me.

High Storrs School was right on top of one of Sheffield's seven hills, brutally exposed to the elements. In winter we used to shiver high up there on the playing fields. Once finished and inside, the first thing you wanted to do was jump in a hot shower. I remember coming home after football with chilblains on my hands almost every week. It toughened us up, though.

Having my dad as a teacher had its plus points, too. Since he had started working there before I was a pupil, I got to know the school inside out while I was still at primary school. I'd walk up Ringinglow Road from Ecclesall Junior School and hang out with him well before I was old enough to attend. I'd sometimes play sport with older kids after school when my dad was coaching them. I was team mascot for my dad's sixth-form football team which won the Yorkshire Cup one year. Mascot status even gave me my first chance to drive a car when my dad used to let me sit on his knee and steer his car around the massive school playing field. (Not that this nurtured my driving skills in any way, as you'll discover later.) So when I finally started at High Storrs School, I already felt at home there. If your dad's a teacher you risk getting teased but there's no chance you'll ever get bullied.

Whatever sport he put his mind to, my dad was a brilliant coach. Before my club (Hallamshire Tennis & Squash Club) even had a junior coaching programme, it was he who first ran the coaching sessions for kids. In fact, he helped the head pro working there now, John Mullins, to learn squash. My dad knew an immense amount about the sport despite the fact he had never played to a particularly high level. He was a solid club player but never what you'd call a great player. Yet he became an expert in every aspect of the sport. He coached, he sold rackets, he learned how to do a wicked restring, he even ran the club itself for a while, and now he has ended up happy in retirement, running the Hallamshire sports shop. He still plays squash a few times a week. But not in the club leagues or anything at that level. He always chooses the same opponents because he's confident he can beat them. I'm not the only one in my family with a competitive streak.

It was football that was my dad's real sport, though. In his younger days he played semi-professional for non-league teams such as Sutton Town, Alfreton Town and Buxton. He still has the enormous calves to prove it. Alongside his competitive streak, I like to think calf muscles are one of the great things I've inherited from my old man.

He reckons his best season was at Sutton Town when, despite being right-footed, he played on the left wing as part of a deadly 4-3-3 formation. The centre forward was a big target man called Mick Raynor who would cause havoc in the penalty area whenever a cross came in. My dad's job was to get in and around Mick to put away any knock-downs. He reckons he must have scored more than 20 goals that season thanks to Big Mick. Then again, much like my granddad, he is prone to the odd exaggeration. He even still keeps a newspaper clipping at home. "Goal Machine Matthew", reads the headline. You can tell by my perfect recall of all the crucial details that I have heard this story more than a few times.

In an individual sport like squash, parents can make the lousiest coaches. There's too much emotion going on. The relationship between coach and player is way too intimate, way too passionate. It's almost impossible for them to take a step back and see the bigger picture. Yet my dad always seemed to be an exception to this rule. For years during my junior career he was often the person who would talk to me in between games, and still to this day he is one of my main advisers. At all times he was level-headed. He never applied too much pressure – as sports parents are wont to do – but he always insisted that whatever I did in sport I did it properly and assiduously. The only time we fell out was when my effort levels weren't high enough. It didn't matter whether I won or lost. It didn't even matter if I played poorly. It was all about my application levels. We used to have this saying about "applying the 3 Ds": Discipline, Determination and Dedication. I know this makes him sound like he was properly intense, like a pushy parent, but he really wasn't. These were simply the principles that my dad abided by and, in time, I came to respect and abide by them myself. The only time I got into big trouble was if I didn't apply maximum effort. And you can understand why. He was giving up his evenings and weekends, driving me halfway across the country, paying for petrol and hotels, all to further my education on the squash court. If I didn't, in turn, try my hardest, he would rightly get pretty annoyed. He always had a brilliant way of turning things round, though, so that I would become more disappointed in myself than he was in me. I used to hate this feeling. For this reason it was rare that I didn't bust a gut on the court.

My dad was never particularly effusive with his praise, even when I'd played a blinder. (I suppose he is a typically understated Englishman, maybe even a typical Yorkshireman. He's been living in Sheffield for so long now – since university to be exact.) But he was like that with everyone, not just me. Touring professionals based at Hallamshire would often search him out after a good win to see if they might finally elicit a compliment from my old man. He would usually reply with something along the lines of: "Your opponent's rubbish. I can beat him easily". Of course he couldn't beat him easily. It was just his way of keeping people on their toes.

For years my dad and I had this running joke that would take place every year without fail on my birthday. He would hand me a birthday card. I knew what would be written inside: "Happy birthday, son. About time you won something this year." It was the same message even if I'd enjoyed a stunning year on the court.

It's a great example of how he could be stern but with a bit of underlying humour to take the sting off it. It was his way of telling me that I still had to work bloody hard. Even if I was thoroughly satisfied with the year I'd had, he would be instructing me never to rest on my laurels. This continued all throughout my 20s. Even when I started winning Professional Squash Association (PSA) titles and my ranking was edging towards the world top 10, he would still write the same message.

It wasn't until I reached the age of 31, with a World Open title, two Commonwealth gold medals and a world No.1 ranking to my name, that the message changed and he finally stopped telling me it was "about time" I won something. If I remember rightly, that year the message read: "Happy birthday, son. You HAVE won a few things this year. Well done. Love, Dad." I guess the joke had run its course. Or maybe he figured that when your son is the top-ranked player on the planet, that kind of psychology is no longer necessary.

But this year, on my birthday, he revived the joke. I had perhaps my most barren season for a few years and was starting to question whether, at 33, I still had what it takes to be a champion. My dad wrote simply: "Happy birthday, Nick. Remember, Hashim Khan didn't win a British Open title until he was 35."

***

My dad's entire life revolved around sport. As well as teaching PE at school, he would then run all the after-school sports clubs. He even sometimes managed a semi-professional football team at the weekends. Given his chosen subject, he initially had no marking to do after school hours. But towards the end of his teaching career he taught sports studies at A-level, giving him loads of after-school admin as well as the sports clubs. He loved his job.

Where my dad and I bonded the most was Monday nights when the quiz show A Question of Sport came on BBC1. We were religious about watching it. This was in the days when Bill Beaumont and Emlyn Hughes were the team captains. Emlyn was a particular favourite of ours since he played squash and racketball at Hallamshire and was usually found socialising at the club bar afterwards. Watching that TV show was one of the most important rituals in our father-and-son relationship. My granddad would often join in, too. When I was a kid, I think we only ever missed a handful of episodes. We used to compete just as the contestants on the show did. I would keep a tally of who between us had supplied the most correct answers. My dad and granddad were utter sports enthusiasts and it was always pretty close but they could never beat me. Later, when They Think It's All Over started broadcasting, we would always tune in for that show, too.

When I admit to being a sports anorak, I'm not exaggerating. I have this insatiable thirst for sports knowledge. Pick up a newspaper and I automatically turn straight to the back pages. I'll glance at what's on the front but it generally just depresses me. With the board game Trivial Pursuit, I always win the orange pie just a few minutes into the game and then spend the following four hours trying to get the other colours. Pete, my dad's best mate from university, who is a regular winner at pub quizzes, says if he ever made it onto Who Wants to Be a Millionaire? he would choose me as his Phone a Friend. He'd be unwise to call me for anything except a sports question, however.

In 2012 I had the sports anorak's ultimate dream: I got invited to be on the panel of A Question of Sport. I was on ex-England rugby captain Matt Dawson's team, alongside ex-Manchester United footballer Gary Pallister. On the other team with ex-England cricketer Phil Tufnell were the world champion 400 metre hurdler Dai Greene and Welsh rugby international Dwayne Peel. It was the first time a squash player had featured on the show since Peter Nicol's heyday back in the early 2000s.

I'd arrived back in the UK the morning of the show, having just competed in the North American Open in Richmond, Virginia. As you can imagine, I had vicious jet lag. We were due to film A Question of Sport at the BBC's new MediaCityUK, in Salford, at 8pm. I was desperate to get some sleep so I could be on fire and show off my sporting knowledge. Luckily I managed four hours of shut-eye before the BBC car arrived to pick me up. It wasn't my usual method of coping with jet lag, and I knew my sleep patterns for the rest of the week would be all messed up but I didn't care. I felt ready to perform.

There was a great atmosphere in the green room before the show, everyone chatting and drinking beer. We'd all had our make-up done. Mine was caked on so, when we finally walked out into the studio, I looked a bit like Gary Lineker on Match of the Day.

With A Question of Sport, it's a myth that the producers tell you in advance what the questions are going to be. You haven't got a clue. None of the contestants are actors, so it's crucial they look genuinely puzzled when Sue Barker reads them out. However, the producers do ask you not to rattle off the answers too quickly – you've got to play to the crowd a little bit.

So when my first squash question came up – Who won bronze in women's singles at the 2006 Commonwealth Games in Melbourne? – I hesitated for a few seconds, even though I knew instantly it was the New Zealander Shelley Kitchen. I was impressive on other sports, too, even getting a couple of Gary Pallister's football questions for him. So impressive, in fact, that minutes into the show, Matt Dawson asked me to make a return appearance in the future. An honour, indeed.

The contest was neck and neck between the two teams with everything to play for on the final quick-fire round. Sue needed us to come up with sportsmen who had alliterative names. One of them was the French squash player Gregory Gaultier, which I nailed. The final question was: "Name the Welsh rugby international who played number 8 for both his country and The British Lions". Just too late, I realised it was Colin Charvis. But I failed to yell it out in time. In the end that lost us the game overall. I'm still waiting for that call back from Matt Dawson.

***

Consider this: of the 12 men that have ever walked on the surface of the Moon, all of them were either only children or first-born sons. Is that coincidence, or do their achievements have something to do with the nurture and attention they received from their parents?

I've no idea. I'm no expert on child-rearing. (Not yet, anyway.) However, I am an only child. That must have had a bearing, somewhere along the line, on my sporting ability and psychology.

Some of the world's greatest sportspeople have been only children: Tiger Woods, Maria Sharapova, Nick Faldo... Then again, most of the world's greatest sportspeople are NOT only children.

Elvis Presley, Frank Sinatra and John Lennon were only children. Paul McCartney, Mick Jagger and Madonna are not. Isaac Newton and Leonardo da Vinci were only children. Albert Einstein and Pablo Picasso were not. All of which goes to prove one thing: maybe being an only child helps you excel in your chosen field; maybe it doesn't. Who knows?

One thing I do know, however, is that I personally had a wonderful upbringing. You couldn't ask for better parents than my mother and father. (And I'm not just saying that because I know they're reading this with pride.) You weren't perfect, Mum and Dad, but you were pretty close.

I was born in July 1980, in Jessop Hospital, in the centre of Sheffield. Since that auspicious day the building has been variously demolished or subsumed as part of Sheffield University. I'm a Leo, an only child and a Yorkshireman. I'm not really sure what that combination means but it sounds like a lethal cocktail that ought really to spontaneously combust. I sometimes think my whole life so far has been one long but gradual spontaneous combustion.

As an only child, inevitably there's a lot more attention lavished on you. I was spoilt but only in a good way. When there aren't other siblings to consider, parents have to be prudent not to let you always get your own way. Fortunately I was never spoilt rotten and I hope I never had the attitude that you sometimes see in only kids from very rich families. I have this image in my head of that character from Charlie and the Chocolate Factory. Her name was Veruca Salt and she was the most over-indulged, obnoxious child you could ever meet. I may have been, to a certain degree, doted on by my parents but I can safely say I never strayed into Veruca Salt territory. (Actually, perhaps I did on the odd occasion.)

When it came to sport, I had a major advantage. My parents were able to focus a huge amount of time and effort on my squash. They both had full-time jobs but at weekends they would gladly ferry me to and from tournaments. My squash became their hobby, too.

I grew up in a lovely Victorian townhouse in south Sheffield, in a little village called Nether Edge. We were by no means rich (both parents were teachers) but we were comfortable. The house was spread across four floors in a good neighbourhood. I remember keeping fit by bounding up all those flights of stairs, usually three or four steps at a time.

Growing up, I rarely felt like an only child. There were always people staying at our house: other squash players, school friends, foreign exchange teachers from my mum's school. Often more than one house guest at a time. My surrogate brother was my granddad who lived with us from when I was two and a half years old until after I left home at the grand old age of 24. Ronald Angus Matthew was his name and he was as much a part of my life as my mum and dad were. Because he was always around – after school, at weekends, during the holidays – he became my best friend.

We did everything together. Our various pastimes pretty much revolved around sport. We played cricket, football, rugby, badminton, mini-golf and croquet in the back garden. It was important that each sport should revolve around serious competition, always governed by strict rules. Sometimes, on a Sunday night, my granddad and I would team up against my dad to play American football after we'd been watching it on TV. Or we would dress up in the Calgary Flames ice hockey shirts that my great aunt had sent me from Canada and then hit pucks up and down the hallway. My mum was never particularly happy about the carnage we caused with that game.

We would play sports video games. We watched sport on TV. I remember once we even set up our own make-believe business where we opened a sports equipment shop in my bedroom. We took it all quite seriously, devising stock takings, price lists and business tactics. Anyone who visited the house had to come up to our shop and buy something. We called it Granick Sports – "Gran" from my granddad, and "Nick" from… well, you get the picture. When you're 10 years old that kind of stuff is fantastic.

My granddad was something of a legend at the junior squash tournaments. All the kids on the junior circuit, even those who didn't know him that well, called him "Granddad". He played rugby quite seriously in his younger days, growing up in South

Wales and competing as scrumhalf for Penarth. He even played on a winning team against the Barbarians and insisted that if international matches hadn't been cancelled during World War II he would definitely have been called up for the Wales national team. He remained a lifelong supporter of Welsh rugby, always standing up for the national anthem whenever Wales played on TV.

I often wonder if, without my granddad, I might have been more of a Veruca Salt-style only child. In my family, not only was I the only child but I was a decade younger than any of my cousins and a decade older than any of my cousins' kids. So I was the golden child; the sole family representative of my generation. (I've lost count how many times I was pageboy at family weddings.) Fortunately, having my granddad around the whole time stopped me becoming utterly self-absorbed.

He was incredibly sporty for his age. When he moved in with us he was already 70 years old yet he'd be out in the garden with me at any opportunity, bowling googlies, kicking penalties, sinking 10 foot putts and walloping me with rugby spin passes. I got my own back, though. Any time I was up to bat I'd smash the ball over the hedge and score 10 runs while he jogged off reluctantly to fetch it.

Like all granddads, my one had some legendary stories he liked to tell. A bit like Uncle Albert from Only Fools and Horses, he was prone to the odd bit of repetition and exaggeration. In his earlier days he had been a personal assistant to the production manager for the Hawker Siddeley aircraft manufacturers. He would constantly remind me how he used to train before work every morning – 1,000 skips on the skipping rope, a two-mile run to the local swimming pool, a 1,000-metre swim, a run back home and 100 press-ups before then heading off to work. The exercise reps increased with every telling of the story.

Another favourite of his involved how quickly he could drive from Rugby, where he lived at the time, to our house in Sheffield. Every Christmas, as he recounted the story, his journey time would decrease by five minutes. It started off taking an hour. Several years later he'd progressively shaved it down to 20 minutes. Bear in mind it's 88 miles from Rugby to Sheffield. To do that in 20 minutes he'd have to be driving at 264mph. Not bad work.

Of all my grandparents, my granddad featured the most. I was close to my mum's mum, who lived near Leeds, but she passed away in my teenage years. My other grandparents both died when I was younger whereas my paternal granddad soldiered on until I was 27, to the ripe old age of 94. He was very much the family patriarch, especially after he moved in with us and brought the entire extended family – all my uncles and aunts – much closer together.

And he was a picture of health, right into his 90s. Even then people would mistake him for a 70-year-old. He had broken his back in his 70s, falling backwards off a wall while tending my grandma's grave, yet even after that he seemed to be back up and running in no time. Then, suddenly, after he had a fall in the kitchen at the age of 92, he aged instantly. It was a big shock to all of us. Knowing how stubborn and determined he was, we all expected him to make the big 100. Unfortunately he was bed-ridden for his final couple of years. We rearranged our downstairs dining-room so that he could stay on the ground floor and my Auntie Sue worked her nursing connections to make sure carers could visit him every day.

Despite his relative youthfulness, he was always convinced he was older than he was. Whenever anyone asked he'd always tell them he was 100. It had been his big goal to reach his century and we didn't want him to give up on life. We were worried that if he really believed he was 100 years old he'd stop fighting and gradually slip away. So we'd always challenge him about his age. "Where's your letter from the Queen, then, Granddad?" I'd say. "Oh, it's around here somewhere," he'd answer, quick as a flash. But it was just another one of his embellished stories. What I wouldn't give now to hear one of those stories again.

All that time spent with my granddad makes me sound like I had no friends of my own age. Actually, being an only child, I often invited kids to our house. Good friends Richard and Edward were two boys who lived next door. I'd often go round to theirs to hone my computer-game skills but they weren't that sporty, so when it came to playing sport I was much better off with my dad or granddad. My closest friends of all were Tom and Paul, the kids of my parents' best friends from university, Pete and Jan. Every year we'd all go off on our summer holidays together, usually to the sports resort Club La Santa, in Lanzarote. Here we could play every sport under the sun to our heart's content.

I'm now godfather to Paul's daughter Maggie. It was thanks to Tom and Paul's father, Pete, that I first took up squash. All the way back in 1975, before squash was even a twinkle in my eye, Pete invited my mum and dad to join him and Jan for a game at his local club – Stocksbridge Leisure Centre, on the outskirts of Sheffield. My mum, dad and Jan loved it so much that they signed up for a beginner's course the following week. Pete, being Pete, thought he was too good for that and signed up for the intermediate course.

It turns out I have a lot to be thankful to Pete for. He passed on the squash bug to my parents and they in turn passed it on to me. You could say Pete is responsible for my whole squash career. Pete and Jonah Barrington, to be precise. It was around this time – in the mid-1970s, that Jonah more or less single-handedly pioneered the squash boom that eventually swept the nation. Pete, however, is convinced he was the catalyst for my squash career and he never fails to remind me of that. When I reached the world No.1 spot, he sent me a birthday card saying: "Don't forget who is the real number 1, Nicky Boy!"

What about my mum, then? I can't possibly leave her out of this story. She'd never forgive me. Sue is a very softly-spoken lady, the calmest character you could ever meet. I can safely say my hotheadedness comes from my dad's side. When I feel the need to smooth things over after an argument, that comes from my mum's side.

I may be in my mid-30s now but my mum still plays a major role in my life. Sometimes embarrassingly so. She and my dad live just 10 minutes away so she's often round, checking up on my domestic set-up. It's hard to believe but she insists on doing the cleaning. I can well afford to hire a cleaner of my own but she won't hear of it. It's all part of her need to help people, much like she cared so much for my granddad and, more specifically, her need to dote upon her only son.

She was always like that. I suppose it's part of her teaching gene. She used to teach English literature at Wickersley School & Sports College, out past Rotherham, to the east of Sheffield. This, of course, meant my grammar, spelling and handwriting as a kid were always up to scratch. Compare that to quite a few professional sportsmen who can barely string three words together. I've never been a keen reader of books, however. I've never, like my mum, had a passion for English literature. Pretty much everything I read is in the back pages of the newspapers, until I go on holiday when I then branch out into sports biographies.

My mum gets very nervous whenever I'm playing a match. My dad can't get enough of professional squash – he has Squash TV piped all day into the Hallamshire club shop where he works and then puts on more matches when he gets home in the evening. So much squash that, in fact, he might possibly know more about my rivals' playing styles than my own coach DP does. So he always loves watching me compete live. My mum, on the other hand, gets so apprehensive that, if I'm in a major final, she finds it difficult to sleep the night before.

She gets so nervous while I'm actually competing that, often, my dad chooses to sit on the other side of the bleachers from her. Otherwise she'll start to stress him out, too. In 2005, after I beat Lee Beachill at the English Open in Sheffield, my mum was more emotionally unstable than I'd ever seen her. Lee had recently topped the world rankings and was still one of the strongest players in the world. That night I beat him from two games down, something that had never happened to Lee before. My mum – bless her – had got herself so worked up during my win that her brain can't have been functioning properly. Leaving the car park of the Crucible Theatre afterwards, she crashed her car. That's how emotional she gets.

Both my parents come to nearly all of my UK matches and, on top of that, they fly out to at least one tournament abroad each year. They have been to New York, Cairo, Doha and Bermuda to support me. Not a bad retirement hobby, I suppose. It's always a massive pleasure having them there with me. Some parents of the professional players I know have never, or, at best, very rarely seen their sons or daughters play. So I feel very privileged to have always had such supportive parents. I never feel any pressure playing in front of them. It's my mum who feels the pressure when she's watching me.

CHAPTER 2

Snoring rhinos

In which we find Nick wearing his squash shorts pulled
up round his nipples, injuring his hands playing knuckles,
and sharing stories of soiled clothing.

My dad's sleeping next to me in the double bed. My granddad's
kipping on the sofa. Both of them are snoring like rhinos and I can't
get a wink of sleep.

This is my abiding memory of my days as a junior player. My
dad, my granddad and I would drive all over the UK so that I could
compete in various tournaments. To save money we'd all bunk up
in the one room at some fine roadside hotel. Travelodges and Little
Chef restaurants did a roaring trade thanks to us.

I remember having a huge map of the UK on my bedroom wall
with pins stuck into every town I'd played in. By the end of my
junior career it looked like a hedgehog. Sometimes I wish, as a senior
player, I'd done the same with a world map. It's easy to forget just
how many places on this planet I've now competed in.

My first ever junior tournament was the Huddersfield Open
under 10s event in 1989. I was nine at the time and one of the
best players in my age group at my club. I remember arriving in
Huddersfield confident I could do really well. Sure enough, I made
it through to the semi-final. Then, suddenly, I got the biggest eye-
opener a slightly cocky youngster could get. I found myself up
against a lad from Collingham, near Leeds, called Jonathan Smith.
He was no taller than me, and actually slightly younger but, boy,
could he play squash. He walloped me 9-0, 9-0, 9-0. (Back in those
days we used traditional scoring to nine points where you would
score only when you were serving. Now on the professional tour

we play point-per-rally to 11 points.) I could barely get Jonathan's crafty lob serve back, never mind win a point. In fact, he went on to become my nemesis in the junior game for the next six or seven years.

Since I was an only child, the junior tournaments I enjoyed the most were when we all teamed up for the Yorkshire county team. We had some great players: the aforementioned Jonathan Smith (who later won British junior titles at under 12 and under 14), Neil Guirey (who is now head pro at Abbeydale, in Sheffield, my secondary coach and my best friend), and James Willstrop (one of my rivals at the top of the world rankings). As Yorkshire, we used to take on other British regions. So, Kent, Surrey and Sussex, for example, would team up to form London & the Southeast, while Cheshire, Lancashire and Merseyside would combine as the Northwest. We often won those encounters. One year when there was a dispute over the home nation internationals, Yorkshire had to step in to replace the England team. Despite being only one county, we beat all the other home nations 5-0.

Jonathan Smith, as you can imagine, was always Yorkshire No.1, while Neil and I would always play second and third fiddle. The only player anywhere close to Jonathan was a young left-hander from Kent called Adrian Grant. In most of the Yorkshire junior tournaments Neil and I would invariably meet in the semi-finals on the Sunday morning so that, by the time we had knocked ten bells out of each other, the winner wouldn't stand a chance against Jonathan in the afternoon. I remember the first time I ever beat Jonathan like it was yesterday. My dad was proud of all the fitness work he had done with me and, for that reason, always maintained that my first victory over Jonathan would be from 2-0 down. He was right. It was the Ilkley Junior Open and I had managed somehow to beat Neil 3-0 in the semi-finals. The extra energy this gave me meant I was able to come back in the final against Jonathan later that day. I was 15 at the time. It was six long years since that 9-0, 9-0, 9-0 drubbing he had given me on our first encounter.

Despite being one of the best players in my county and a member of England junior squads from the age of 14, I never won a British national title as a junior. Yet, as a senior, I reached world No.1. This proves that you don't have to be the best as a youngster in your chosen sport in order to have a successful career in the seniors. I believe this applies to just about any sport and is a valuable lesson for all aspiring youngsters. I was never a particularly talented junior player and lost count of the number of times I was told I would never make it as a professional. I was accused of wasting my time. Apparently there were kids with much more talent than I had. But where are those kids now?

If you're willing to work hard enough, and for a long enough period of time, it doesn't matter that you're not at the top of your sport as a junior. There is no limit to what can be achieved. Sometimes I think it was a blessing in disguise that I didn't have it all my own way when I was younger. It made me hungrier for success, and made me appreciate success all the more when I finally achieved it.

Looking back at the photos of me as a junior player, one thing strikes me in particular. I always used to wear my shorts pulled right up above my waist, with my shirt tucked right in. I looked like a total geek. My other problem was that I couldn't take the mickey out of myself – a serious disadvantage when you're part of a junior squad. I'll admit that, at that tender age, I hadn't developed a sense of humour. You can imagine how I suffered at the hands of the other players.

When I was 15 I went to Welwyn Garden City, in Hertfordshire, for a nationals squad. One morning, all the other kids walked in, laughing, with their shorts pulled right up over their nipples. I couldn't handle it when I quickly realised they were mocking me so I pretended my back was hurting and cried off the training session, skulking back to the hotel. Like the spoilt only child I was, I assumed the other kids were really picking on me when in fact it was all just part of the normal squash team banter. To add insult to injury (literally), I was nursing sore hands from the night before after playing that vicious knuckle-rapping game teenagers so love. I'd come off the worst and the tops of my hands were bleeding. (Not the smartest game to play when you're training for racket sports.) So I was really feeling sorry for myself that day. But at least I learned one valuable lesson: from then on I tried to wear my shorts well below my waist and my shirt untucked. I wasn't quite what you'd call cool but I was trying.

Junior squash teaches you some invaluable lessons that arm you for the rigours of the senior tour. In 1995 I won my first major junior tournament – the Spanish Junior Open. In the draw there were something like 20 kids from the same private school in Gloucestershire – Wycliffe College. En route to the title I'd had to take on four of them and for each match the rest of the Wycliffe squad turned out to cheer on their teammate. By the time I'd reached the final I felt like things were getting a little bit personal. Every point I won, there was silence. Every point I lost, the crowd erupted in shouts and screams.

Professional footballers say that a hostile crowd of 100 people is much more difficult to deal with than one of 60,000 people because in a small crowd you can hear exactly what they're shouting. It was like that when I took on those boys from Wycliffe College. But I won the tournament. And it prepared me for the belligerent spectators I'd meet later in my career.

The highlight of my junior career was winning the British Junior Open in early 1999 in my home town of Sheffield, beating the then world junior champion Ong Beng Hee in the final. Actually, Beng Hee never made it as far as the court, succumbing to a bout of food poisoning the night before. I suppose I have the Sheffield chefs to thank for that but it certainly wasn't the way I wanted to win such a prestigious event. It is so far the only final in the event's entire illustrious history that has been won by default.

Junior squash also teaches you how to compete in team events. One of the most memorable was the World Junior Team Championships in 1998, at Princeton University, in New Jersey. There were five of us on the squad – me, Adrian Grant, Lee Jemmett (this crazy kid from Essex), Jonathan Kemp and Ben Garner. Jonathan and Ben had been ill all week with food poisoning.

With all the world's top juniors in attendance, it was a great atmosphere. The French team – Gregory Gaultier, Romain Tenant and Nicolas Siri (who tragically died on court a few years later of heart complications) – all dyed their hair the colours of the French flag, one red, one white and one blue.

The Pakistani team had one player, Mohammed Hussain, who was clearly much older than 18. There's a big problem in junior squash with some of the Pakistani and Egyptian players who fail to produce valid birth certificates and end up competing in age groups below their actual age. Mohammed swore he was 18 but he sported a full bushy moustache at the time. We used to joke that he had a wife and kids waiting for him back home. I think he was closer to 26 than 18. Despite the fact that he was much bigger than me, I confronted him at the post-tournament dinner, demanding to know why, since he was in his mid-20s, he couldn't beat a bunch of juniors and win the tournament. He obviously took exception to this because the next time I played him, six months later, was on the professional tour and he drilled me in the calf with the ball twice in quick succession as hard as he could. (I probably deserved it for being such a big mouth but I must have been correct about his age since, six years later, he had retired from the sport.)

By the end of that week, we'd reached the junior team final against Egypt. I managed to beat Mohammed Abbas but Adrian Grant lost to Wael El Hindi, setting up a deciding match between Lee Jemmett and future world No.1 Karim Darwish. Lee won't mind me saying that, at the time, he was prone to get a bit chubby if he didn't eat or train properly. But at that tournament he was in the best shape of his life. Karim was two years younger than Lee and had lost to him in the pool stages of the tournament, chalking up only a handful of points in the process. We all therefore assumed Lee was a shoo-in for the final.

By the end of the week, with limited laundry services, we'd pretty much run out of clean kit. The plan was, though, to all wear the same Adidas shorts for the final. Lee's were all dirty so he was forced to borrow a pair from food-poison boys Jonathan and Ben, who were sharing a room. Holding his breath, and fearful he might succumb to their bacteria, he went to their room to search out some clean shorts. Inside it looked like they'd had a break-in. You couldn't actually see the floor for discarded clothes. The stench of illness made his eyes water. The only Adidas shorts he could find bore the battle wounds of John's multiple visits to the toilet. This was a team effort, though, so Lee didn't complain. He bravely pulled on those shorts and stepped out on court for the final.

By God, did he put us through the wringer during that match. It lasted an hour and a half, with every moment utter agony to watch. (Perhaps those shorts were worse than we'd initially imagined.) Lee was incredibly nervous and lost the first game 9-7. He won the next 9-2 and we thought everything was on track, only for him to lose the third 9-4. He regrouped and won the fourth 9-1 and then the match see-sawed all the way through the fifth until it was 9 points apiece. They then traded match points before Lee eventually closed out the match. I was on the front row with Adrian and we exploded with joy when Lee finally won. We were so excited, leaping so high on match point, that we actually split the bleacher we were sitting on.

That night was one of the first times in my life that I got properly drunk. I'll admit I'm a bit of a lightweight when it comes to alcohol and the fact that we'd been sitting in a hot sports arena all evening after having hard matches must have helped my inebriety on its way. Not to mention the emotional turmoil Lee had put us through. Being 18, we were too young to drink legally in the United States. Somewhere on the university grounds we sniffed out a fraternity party – you know those American college parties with preposterous amounts of beer and raucous drinking. Since we were English and we'd just won the championship, we were immediately invited in. Apart from confronting Mohammed and trying to throw an American football at Greg Gaultier's bleached red head (and failing miserably), I remember very little of that night.

Like all teenagers, we seemed to spend a lot of our spare time seeking alcohol, even though it wreaks havoc with your body and your squash the next day. My last ever junior tournament was the European Championships in Vienna. It was the first time the World Squash Federation decreed that juniors had to compete wearing goggles. I'd rarely worn them before and wasn't used to the way they sit tight against your face. There was the added problem that I sweat a lot from my head. The goggles quickly filled with my sweat and steamed up so I could barely see the ball. I also buckled under the pressure and, despite being top seed, reached only the semi-finals, losing to a much younger Gaultier. Adrian Grant won the title.

Adrian and I got in a spot of bother in Vienna. Somehow we managed to get hold of the master key for all the rooms in the hotel we were staying in. For several days, in between matches, we would wander into empty rooms and avail ourselves of the mini-bar contents and porn channels. A teenager's dream.

We were getting away with it handsomely until we accidentally barged in on a couple who were asleep. Then someone reported a watch missing and we were accused of theft. Things got really hairy then. (We were innocent, by the way.) The chief executive of England Squash demanded that Adrian and I were ejected from the National Lottery funding programme. Our parents received stern letters. England Squash had to pay for all the whiskey and porn we'd consumed. It was only a couple of years ago that I found out DP had put in a good word for us and managed to smooth things over. A good job, too. It's possible I never would have made it as a professional player without Lottery funding.

CHAPTER 3

The gaffer

In which a youthful Nick upsets older players, falls
asleep on the Snake Pass, disappoints in his A-levels and
introduces us to his greatest fan.

There have been two great coaches in my life. For the last 14 years
DP has been my right-hand man. But during my formative years,
from the age of 10 to 19, it was Mark Hornby. Mark knew squash
inside out, brilliant at both the tactical and physical side of the
sport. Without him there's no way I would be the player I am today.

We first met at Abbeydale Park Rackets & Fitness Club, near
where I grew up in Sheffield. Head pro there, he obviously spotted
some vague spark of talent in me because he offered to coach me
for a really decent rate. Sometimes my granddad would pay him for
my lessons. Other times I would work for Mark in return for free
coaching. I'd babysit his kids. I'd help him in the club shop. Or I'd
sweep the courts or string rackets for him.

My racket stringing skills were appalling so he didn't get much
of a bargain out of that particular reciprocal agreement. For the
unversed, racket stringing can be quite complicated. You have to
thread the strings in the right order, at the right tension and tie them
off at the right grommet. Yes, it's tricky, especially when you're a
little kid who just wants to get out on the court and play. I'll admit
I did some horrendous string jobs with the wrong stringing pattern,
the incorrect tension and too many knots. Pity the poor members
at Abbeydale who had to use the rackets I'd got my mitts on. But it
earned me free lessons with Mark.

He was a superb coach. As a professional player, in the late
1980s, he was probably one of the best 50 players in the world. (The

rankings system worked very differently back then.) When I met him his real ambition was to guide a player to the top of the world rankings. With me he always had one eye on the future, teaching me to be a good senior player rather than a good junior player. In this sport there are certain shortcuts you can take to make yourself a successful junior, but you risk instilling bad habits that won't help you when you eventually transfer to the senior game. Mark knew that better than anyone.

Among other things, Mark taught me how to volley – still one of my strongest weapons – and how to play a great lob, one of the most under-used and under-appreciated shots in the game. I have him to thank for my attritional game and my fitness. He was a stickler for stretching. Reminding me of his dodgy back and hips – a legacy from his years of playing professionally as sports science wasn't as apparent back then – he would insist that I stretched properly both before and after training. Sometimes I'd come off court, knackered to death, desperate to get back to my mum's home cooking. Yet he'd force me to warm down. "You don't want to end up like me," he'd say, as he hobbled around the club. It was an unbelievable education.

One of the most valuable periods of my junior days was when Mark took me with him to play in county league matches. Every Tuesday night we'd drive over the Pennines to Bolton to play for Eagley Squash Club in the Northwest Counties League (Mark was originally from Rochdale in Lancashire). He would normally come in as a ringer at number five and I would get some great experience playing at number two behind full-time pro player Marcus Berrett.

I was 15 and 16 years old at the time and these were tough no-prisoners adult leagues. In those days I used to spend most of my free time slugging out matches. Some weeks I'd be playing for Hallamshire in the Sheffield & District League on a Monday night, Eagley on a Tuesday, and Hallamshire again in the Yorkshire League on a Wednesday. I'd get home late at night with school the next day.

I was a right cocky little so-and-so back then. Many kids who are cocky use it as a front to disguise their fear. That wasn't the case with me. I was just too big for my own boots. I used to infuriate the adult players in that Northwest Counties League. They'd often come off court having lost to me and head straight for Mark, incredulous that I could act so arrogantly on court. On one occasion I beat a well-respected local player 9-0, 9-0, 9-0. It was an easy match and I felt like I hadn't really given myself enough of a workout. So afterwards I sauntered onto the neighbouring court and did a tough ghosting session. Not surprisingly, this really rubbed salt into the wounds of the player I'd just beaten. His name was Brent Sherman. If I'd had any manners at all I would have found a remote court somewhere else in the club. As it was, I might as well have pinned a notice up in the club reception telling everyone Brent was rubbish and that he hadn't made me break a sweat. But because I was so cocky and insensitive, it didn't even occur to me that I was being rude. (Brent, if you happen to read this, I apologise for my appalling manners.) It turned out that Brent was a good friend of Mark's and phoned him at Abbeydale the next morning to complain about my behaviour. I'm sure that during those two seasons Mark had to field quite a few such calls on Wednesday mornings.

I used to get paid around £50 a night for those league matches which, for a 15-year-old, is a king's ransom. And Mark did all the driving across the Pennines, paid for all the petrol, never asking me to contribute. Those leagues played an invaluable part in my development since I had to take on players bigger than me, stronger than me and much more experienced. Sometimes I would play full-time professional players. And on the journey home to Sheffield, as we drove high up across Snake Pass, Mark would dissect every last shot I'd played that evening. Often it was midnight and I was nodding off in the passenger seat. But I suppose much of his analysis must have sunk into my mind, even just subliminally.

As a kid I'd sometimes get so frustrated with squash that I felt like packing it in altogether. All athletes who make careers out of their sport let those doubts creep into their mind at one time or another. Other times I imagined I was going to be the best player in the world. Yet during that period I wasn't even one of the best juniors in the country, never mind the world. Imagine how big-headed I would have been if I was. I blame it on youthful naivety.

Mark was well aware of my cockiness – he'd seen it in action at those Eagley matches as well as during my junior tournaments – and rightly tried to rein it in. After one training session during which I'd been obnoxiously cocky he turned to me and said: "I don't think you'll require the services of a sports psychologist when you're older." I wasn't sure whether he meant I was a know-it-all, or whether it was a compliment about my mental strength. I decided to accept it as a compliment because you never received many of those from Mark. On the rare occasions when he did applaud your game you knew you'd damn well earned it. He was very similar to my dad in that sense.

The problem was that Mark was incredibly intense. Both as a coach and as a human being, he would get really stressed about various issues. I once visited him in hospital after he had made himself ill through stress. I vividly remember him saying to me, "I bet you never expected to see me in here."

It was just before I was due to fly out to the World Junior Championships in the States in 1998. There were doubts about whether Mark would be well enough to accompany me. But I knew just how determined a human being he was. He was one of the few people I knew as stubborn as me. Sure enough, he made it over to the States and helped me through to the semi-finals of the individual event.

Mark had coached many players in the past who had gone on to successful professional careers. He felt many of them had betrayed him. I'm told some of them left him because he was so possessive, demanding they sign contracts with him. He tried to persuade me to sign a contract, too, guaranteeing him a percentage of my future earnings. I was young at the time and felt trapped by that. I wanted to pay him per coaching session instead.

Mark's insecurity about the player-coach relationship was obvious, and, given the previous betrayals, hardly surprising. He'd often say to me: "You're not just using me, are you, like the other players did? You're not going to leave me, are you?" In some ways it was like having a jealous lover.

Although he was always so generous with his time, and played such a key role in my development, I suppose ultimately his ambition was to gain the reputation of having coached a world-class player. Perhaps he saw me as his ticket to success. I think he had seen how Peter Nicol's coach, Neil Harvey, had his reputation secured for life on the back of Peter's success. Once Peter hit the big time, suddenly Neil found himself surrounded by a pool of players wanting his Midas touch. I think Mark felt my success could have a similar effect on his coaching career.

In the end, working with Mark became an unbearable pressure cooker. We'd do the same training sessions, day in day out, sometimes twice a day. He'd put me under such intense pressure that I'd leave the court a sweating mess. Don't get me wrong: those sessions were amazing for my development as a player, and they made me incredibly strong, but variety in one's training is crucial. I wasn't getting that. Eventually I stopped enjoying it all. I decided to split from Mark and join up with DP instead.

To this day it is the most difficult decision I've ever had to make. DP and Mark, who both grew up in Lancashire, had been best friends earlier in their lives. They had played squash together all the time when they were kids and ended up on the same adult England team. DP was a guest at Mark's wedding. Ironically it had been DP and his brother Brian who had first introduced Mark to squash. When I was 10 years old and my dad was trying to find me a top coach, it was DP who had suggested Mark.

DP had usually got the better of Mark during their playing careers, but when Mark won one of their encounters at Abbeydale in the World Masters Over 35s in 1999 they had a bit of a handbag moment in the locker room afterwards. Their relationship never really recovered after that. In hindsight I think this fallout had been brewing ever since DP was first appointed national coach in 1996, a role Mark had really wanted for himself.

If Mark had been a more laid-back character then perhaps I might have stayed under his tutelage. We were really close for many years but there wasn't much of a relationship between us outside of squash. No release valve for the pressure cooker. Not surprisingly, really, when you consider he was 20 years older than me. Apart from our chosen sport, what else could we possibly have in common?

When I first told Mark I planned to move on it was really strange because he appeared to be thrilled for me. He offered to continue coaching me whenever I wanted to supplement DP's coaching. But I knew I had to make a clean break. For a short overlap period I tried working with both coaches. On court with Mark, though, I could tell instantly he wasn't happy with the situation. We'd train for an hour and he wouldn't utter a word. Afterwards I'd ask him if I was making improvements and he'd just mutter something sarcastic like, "Well, you know what's best for your game..." It was obvious our professional relationship had fizzled right out.

One person who at first wasn't sure whether I'd made the right decision in switching from Mark to DP was my dad. During that period was the only time I ever remember properly falling out with him. He simply couldn't understand what I was feeling inside, all the negative stuff I'd been storing up: my problems with Mark's intensity, the way I wasn't enjoying the sport as much. It was a couple of years before he could see the bigger picture. At the time, all he understood was the exterior stuff like my match results and what my swing looked like.

At first it seemed my dad was correct to have reservations. My ranking stalled; my confidence ebbed away. Occasionally we'd argue over the dinner table about my decision to change my playing style. Mind you, I'm not surprised he was sceptical. DP taught an exaggerated technique so that, for example, to encourage me to stop playing backhands with my elbow so tight to my chest, he would get me to extend my arm right out. Until I'd grown into the new shot, the resulting swing looked ridiculous.

In my early days with DP my squash results plateaued. It took me a while to work out how to remodel my entire technique under his unorthodox coaching style. Mark had been a very physical coach while DP is almost exclusively technical. In the months after switching coaches my dad kept pointing out that I was losing fitness, such was the emphasis on my technical work. It dawned on me that I needed both a coach and a fitness trainer.

That's when I started working regularly with Damon Leedale-Brown from Sheffield Hallam University. Later on I worked with the English Institute of Sport – also in Sheffield – and I've been consulting them for all my off-court fitness ever since. Mark had wanted to be my squash coach, my physical trainer, my psychologist, even my priest. In contrast, DP accepted his limitations. He knew he was a great coach but that other people were more qualified in other areas of the sport. It was back then that I started developing a team of experts around me, like I have today.

It took time, and a lot of faith, for things to work out with DP but I have never had the slightest doubt that I made the right decision. Thankfully, over time, my dad has become DP's biggest fan.

Nowadays Mark is coaching the Norwegian national team. I occasionally bump into him at tournaments on the tour but, apart from a courteous hello, there's no relationship between us. I would love to go out for a drink with him and reminisce over old times. Together we shared some of my greatest moments in squash. All that hard work behind the scenes; the pressure sessions he put me through, each leaving me a dripping mess on the court, trying to suck in air like my life depended on it. Then he would put me back through it all again. Sometimes after those killer sessions it felt like I had to crawl off the court. It really felt like I had sweated blood. The seeds Mark sowed truly shaped me into the player I've become. When you go through those experiences with someone you have such a strong bond.

It's strange that Mark and DP had originally been best mates. Then years later, after they'd fallen out, I would prove to be a further bone of contention between them. One thing I'm sure of, however, is that if I hadn't switched to DP, I would never have become the world's No.1 squash player.

I already knew DP fairly well since he was the national coach for England Squash. The first time I met him was when I was 13 years old and he was helping the then national coach, Paul Wright, with a junior national squad. But it wasn't until I was preparing for the World Junior Championships in 1998 that I really got to know him properly. It was just after I'd sat my A-levels. Unfortunately for my A-levels, my mind was much more on squash than on academic studies. Having trained really hard for the championships, I pretty much ignored my books in the lead-up to my exams. The result was a D in economics, a B in English language, a C in general studies and (most disappointing of all since I was expected to get an A) a B in sports studies.

I really loved sports studies. My special A-level project – which I received top marks for, by the way – was to devise an alternative scoring system for squash. My plan was to make squash more dynamic, more spectator-friendly, more TV-friendly, with loads of exciting and critical points. I took the project really seriously, arranging loads of real tournaments at my club and observing how they played out under the various different scoring systems. (If you're interested, the system that ended up providing the most exciting points was the tennis model.)

I didn't fare anywhere near as well as I would have liked to on my exams, however. But as I flew out to the World Junior Championships, my A-levels were the last thing on my mind. All I was thinking about was turning professional.

It was my first proper experience of DP as a coach. I was instantly impressed by the way he managed all the staff and players, and at the professional yet, crucially, relaxed set-up he had created around him. It was also my first experience of working closely with Damon Leedale-Brown, who accompanied the team. Damon, a sports scientist, introduced me to proper nutrition, hydration, training, match recovery, coping with jet lag – everything that nowadays I take for granted. We also had another coach, Paul Carter, who had guided and prepared the team brilliantly. The whole set-up made us all feel so confident and so professional that we played out of our skins, beating Egypt in the final. Less than a year later I had joined forces with DP permanently.

He's a very relaxed, easy-going sort of guy, a quality that must have seemed even more attractive to me at first after all the intensity and pressure I'd felt with Mark. DP lives in Harrogate with his wife Jo. He has two kids, Emma and James, from his first marriage, and his step-kids, David and Jenny Duncalf.

Squash fans will be well aware of Jenny's exploits on the court. She's an astoundingly good player and like most of DP's pupils has a beautiful technique. Jenny is still inside the world top 10 as I'm writing this, and was up as high as No.2 in the world between 2009 and 2011, winning a silver medal at the 2010 Commonwealth Games. DP coached Jenny from when she first picked up a racket in 1992 right throughout her career, something which can't have been easy considering the father-stepdaughter relationship. But, looking at her results, it obviously worked. Her brother David is also an accomplished player, though not at the same level. I remember playing him many times in the juniors. At the time of writing he works as a coach in Canada.

DP's daughter Emma has cerebral palsy, which confines her to a wheelchair and means she requires almost constant care. She is without doubt my biggest fan. Any time I'm competing in the north of England she will travel to the tournament and cheer me on

Looking hot and bothered post-match with my granddad and biggest supporter at my first international event, the Dutch Junior Open, 1994.

My mum gets a sweaty hug after I win the 2012 British Open at the O2 Arena. My dad was clearly listening to the commentary on Squash TV, or was he listening to his favourite band?

My first England kit arrives in 1995.
Notice how high I wear my shorts
and how knobbly the knees are.

Emma is always present at my biggest
matches, even my biggest match of all:
my and Esme's wedding in 2013.

Troubles brewing on a road trip with the Yorkshire junior team and my best friend
Neil. Modes of transport have improved considerably over the years.

Barcelona 1998, as runner-up in my first ever PSA tournament, Ciutat de Barcelona. Alberto (left) had sacrificed his wildcard place in the event – a massive gesture from a lifelong friend.

My first sponsored car. I could hardly remain inconspicuous or indulge in road rage while driving this.

In 2001 I was starting to get noticed. This is my first appearance on the front cover of a magazine. I'm still waiting to do a cover shoot for Sports Illustrated.

The most iconic squash venue of all time in front of the Great Pyramids of Giza and the unfortunate scene of my breaking wind during a match.

Coach DP struggles to get a word in edgeways as I have a rest between games on my way to winning the World Open in Saudi Arabia in 2010.

This was my breakthrough win as I became the first English winner of the British Open (aka the Wimbledon of squash) for 67 years.

Some pictures tell a thousand words. Joy and despair in equal measures for me and James, and the start of a fractured relationship.

James and I make our infamous phone call to Radio 2 DJ Chris Evans less than an hour before the 2009 British Open final. You can see the tension on both of our faces.

Exulted company indeed. I felt out of place next to such squash legends: (from left) Peter Nicol, Jahangir Khan, Lee Beachill, Hashim Khan, me, Azam Khan, Anthony Rickets, Geoff Hunt.

Off to the beach in Bermuda with regular roommate Adrian Grant. One of my favourite photographs depicting the lighter side of the tour. This time I managed to stay upright on the moped.

Party time, 1st June 2010: Great timing as a lads' holiday in Mexico coincided with the first time I got to world No.1.

A tough taskmaster taking instructions off the toughest of them all. I've learnt over the years to keep quiet and do as Mr. Campbell says.

madly. Her support always gives me an enormous boost. She's been known to scream particularly loudly whenever I'm up against James Willstrop.

Emma is so philosophical about her situation. She's 27 years old and deals with her cerebral palsy without a hint of complaint or self-pity, her personality always shining through. It's obvious how much she loves life and how much she lives it to the full. I know this may sound like a bit of a cliché but Emma really helps me keep my own life in perspective. When I complain about one of life's petty annoyances I think of Emma and what she has to endure day to day. When I'm moaning about stiff muscles, not hitting the ball well, delayed planes or lost luggage... I try to think about what Emma has to deal with. My problems then fade into insignificance. Emma has changed DP's outlook on life, too. Bringing up a child with cerebral palsy is obviously no easy task.

I will say that DP isn't the world's healthiest example of a sports coach. He likes a drink, sometimes enjoys a cheeky smoke and is a tad overweight. Mind you, he's in his 50s now. When he was competing professionally he used to be as skinny as a rake, which might explain why he now has a complex about his weight. He often needs reassurance, asking me if he's looking a bit chubby or if he's lost weight. I normally tell him he hasn't, just to keep him on his toes. If only he would move around a bit more in court sessions. I still call him "the demonstrator" because, if I hit a bad shot during training, he will come to the front of the court to demonstrate the correct shot. "Like this," he says, executing it perfectly. These days he tends to stand in one corner, feeding the balls but barely moving his feet. He hits the ball so sweetly every time but he's so rooted to the spot that he never breaks into a sweat.

DP loves to take the mickey out of me, as you'll discover in the "carrot up your arse" incident, in a later chapter. Even today, after my two World Open titles, he likes to show me up in front of a crowd. We'll be training at his club in Harrogate and perhaps there will be a few people watching from the bleachers. Once he's got an audience, that's when the jibes start coming thick and fast. It's his way of ensuring I don't take life too seriously. For example, I used to grip the racket too tightly and he wanted me to relax my grip. So, he'd say to me (loud enough so all the spectators could hear), "Nick, you're never going to get a girlfriend if you grip the racket so tightly. Don't squeeze too hard and don't squeeze too softly. You've got to caress her just right." Another time he would pull his shorts up to his nipples, taking enormous glee in explaining to his audience how I used to wear them.

You can imagine how hilarious the spectators find this. They'd come along to see a serious top pro in training and, for their troubles, they'd be subjected to DP's jokes.

In the early days I used to spend half the week in Harrogate. I'd drive up on a Sunday evening and stay at DP's house with his family until the Thursday. DP and his wife Jo were so kind to me. I became almost like their adopted son. And I grew very close to their kids.

Training under DP was like a breath of fresh air, just what I needed. I felt free again. My squash was blossoming. The results weren't immediate but I was enjoying being on court again, just like the old days when I was a kid. Little did I know that DP was soon to completely dismantle my entire game.

CHAPTER 4

Delay and deception

In which our hero is driven at speed the wrong way up
an Egyptian dual carriageway, learns the true meaning of
lactic acid, and almost defects to Wales.

It has to be the most iconic squash court ever built. Unfortunately
the Al-Ahram International Squash Tournament no longer exists
but when it was staged on and off in Egypt in the 1990s and 2000s,
it was the most stunning setting a player or spectator could ask for.
The brightly-lit all-glass court was constructed just a few hundred
metres from the Great Pyramids of Giza. Like a spaceship that had
landed in the desert, the court ensured even the most pedestrian
matches felt electric with atmosphere. Then there was the backdrop.
Imagine what it felt like stepping out on court as the sun was setting
over the Giza plateau, the ancient pyramids beautifully spotlit on
the horizon. I used to get goose pimples every time I played there.

My first pyramid experience was in 1999 when Peter Nicol went
on to beat the infamous Egyptian Ahmed Barada in the World Open
final. The entire trip was an enormous eye-opener for me. I was just
19 years old and it was my first time in Egypt. Fortunately, English
player Peter Marshall was on hand to mentor me. He was making his
comeback after several years away from squash with chronic fatigue
syndrome and helped me navigate my way through the vagaries of
Egyptian culture: how to barter for a taxi (believe me, you have to
barter hard); how to minimise the risk of food poisoning (salads
were a no-no); how to remain calm when our taxi driver decided
to take a shortcut by heading full pelt the wrong way down a dual
carriageway. Peter also warned me never to put my hands near my
mouth after touching the money. Not easy for someone whose most

compulsive habit, even today, is biting his fingernails.

That first year I lost in qualifying to the experienced South African Glenn Whittaker. It wasn't until the following year, with goose pimples especially bristling, that I got to play on the iconic glass court. I took on Jonathon Power in the first round. This time I had managed to battle through the qualifying rounds but these were staged on traditional courts at Cairo Stadium. It wasn't until I found myself up against Jonathon, the No.2 seed, that I got my chance to play on the pyramid court.

Peter had prepared me for a lot in Cairo but not even he could prime me to take on Jonathon. Jonathon's use of deception and delay made him, in my opinion, one of the toughest players of all time to read. Deception – for those of you not versed in squash terminology – is when a player feigns to play one type of shot but changes his swing at the last second in order to play an entirely different kind of shot. So you might make a show of winding up for a big forehand drive, for example, but then, at the last possible moment, change it to a drop shot, thereby throwing your opponent off their stride.

Delay, on the other hand, is when you stop yourself from striking the ball until the very last moment in order to place your opponent on the wrong footing. Do it effectively and the other player will transfer their body weight too soon and end up out of position entirely for the resulting shot.

Sometimes players will use delay. Sometimes they will use deception. Jonathon was exceptional in that he would employ both in a single shot. That day I went up against him on the pyramid court, I remember he was making me stop and start like a car backfiring. I couldn't get into any sort of rhythm and the burning of the lactic acid in my legs was like nothing I'd ever experienced before in my life. It was shocking. Sometimes a player can lose accuracy if he tries to be overly deceptive. But not Jonathon. Even his deceptive shots were out of the ordinary. When it comes to deception, most players suggest they're going to hit a drive and then play a drop shot but he did it the other way round: he would suggest he was going for a drop shot before suddenly snapping his wrist through to play a powerful drive. It takes incredible timing and a ridiculous level of skill to achieve that, not to mention forearms the size of my thighs.

I lost three games to love but put up a decent enough show

(before the lactic acid kicked in) to let Jonathon know he would face tougher games against me in the future. That match still remains the best learning experience of my entire professional career.

***

Although I turned professional in 1998, and was a member of senior England squads pretty much straight away, it wasn't until 2003 that I won my first cap for my country. Somehow I failed to persuade the England Squash coaches that I was made of stern enough stuff. The best I could ever do was to be first reserve. I found it really frustrating since it was a major ambition of mine to represent my country. When my major rival James Willstrop was picked ahead of me (and he was three years younger than me), it really rubbed salt into the wound.

Finally, in 2003, I proved my mettle by reaching the quarter-finals of the US Open, beating Simon Parke, a former world No.3, and Ong Beng Hee, the World Junior Champion from my age group, who was by now a top 10 player. It was seen as my breakthrough tournament. Surely the England Squash coaches would pick me now.

My coach, DP, also happened to be the English national coach so it would have smacked of serious nepotism if he had been seen as the man who picked me for the team. The week before the next international tournament in the calendar – The World Team Championships, in Vienna – DP kept me hanging on tenterhooks. He wouldn't reveal whether I had actually won a place on the team or not. Everyone knew it was a 50-50 choice between Simon Parke and me for the last spot. Coincidentally, the week before Vienna, I was due to play Simon in a Yorkshire league match. DP phoned me up and said, "Whatever you do, don't play Simon in the league because it won't look good if you lose to him and then get picked for England". He wasn't exactly confirming that I had a place in the team but as a coded message it seemed pretty obvious to me that I was going to get the call-up.

So the following morning, when I received a letter in the post with an England Squash logo on the envelope, I was delighted. At last, here was my first England cap. I hurriedly slit the letter open and I couldn't believe the words I was reading. "After careful consideration, we've decided not to pick you for the World Team Championships." It was like a kick in the testicles. I was utterly fuming with anger. The rest of that day I spent on the phone and the computer trying to ascertain whether I could switch nationalities and play for Wales instead through my granddad's Welsh connection. Patriotic though I am, I was so incensed at what I saw as a total betrayal that I would have abandoned my loyalty to England and competed for Wales instead. I honestly felt like ripping someone's head off. Preferably DP's.

So when DP phoned me up later that day, you can imagine the shortness of the shrift that I gave him. "What the hell do you want!" were my opening words. He was the last person I wanted to speak to. DP said, "I'm calling to tell you you've been selected to play for England. Congratulations on your first cap."

I was flabbergasted. "I've been going mental all day!" I told him. "After I got that rejection letter this morning I was within millimetres of defecting to Wales. Do you know what turmoil I've been through?"

It turns out that England Squash had sent me the wrong letter. I'd received the rejection letter meant for Nick Taylor. Someone at England Squash had mixed up the two Nicks. Fortunately the selection letters weren't due to go out until the following day so Nick Taylor hadn't actually received my selection letter. Imagine his disappointment if he thought he'd been selected, only to be dropped the same day.

England came in third place in Vienna. It wasn't the result the team wanted but, on my debut, I had a positive week, winning important matches in both the semi-final and the bronze medal play-off.

DP remembers the whole episode for other reasons. He says that telephone conversation we had is the rudest I've ever been to him in my entire life. I know the mix-up with the letters wasn't his fault but I don't really feel guilty about it. When I thought I hadn't been selected I was incandescent with anger.

CHAPTER 5

Vegetables in unsavoury places

In which Nick begins to feel like the Karate Kid and eventually
extricates a vegetable from his backside.

"You play like you've got a carrot stuck up your arse!"

That was DP's first ever technical assessment of my squash. It
wasn't a great start to our working relationship. Especially as I didn't
have much of a sense of humour back then. (Remember the shorts
up to the nipples incident in the juniors?) He says he'll never forget
the look of surprise I gave him at his vegetable comment.

But he was right. I was 19 years old and he had just taken over
as my coach. Each time I hit a shot I'd bend my knees and then,
on the follow-through, I'd stand up rigidly. I had no fluidity, no
core stability. There was no link at all between my hitting the ball
and my movement away from it. I'd yo-yo up and down as I moved
around the court. No wonder I had spent a lot of my junior career
nursing a bad back. I had played some effective squash as a junior
but in hindsight I can see that it was ugly, attritional squash. Both
DP and I knew we had to make some serious changes to my playing
style if I wanted to make a mark on the senior game. And we had to
make those changes quickly.

The result was that, in time, I became a totally different squash
player. DP stripped back my game to its raw basics, dismantling my
technique and reteaching me every shot I thought I already knew.
He took me apart and then, piece by piece, he completely rebuilt
me. Nowadays, if I ever look back at video clips of me on court
as a teenager, I cringe. It looks like another player out there. The
difference is that marked.

We used to spend hours analysing my game with a video camera.

Stafford Murray, from the England Institute of Sport, would come and film me training. I'd hit backhand drives down the wall for two hours, stopping after every 20 shots to watch the video and make tiny adjustments. It was a slow, painstaking process (even more so for Stafford) but ultimately it transformed me into a technically much stronger player. It took its toll psychologically, though. Those video sessions were much tougher than any physical workout I've ever done. You won't believe the mental anguish involved in completely relearning the sport I'd been trying to perfect all my life. Everything was so habitual to me. I first learned to play squash at the age of eight and then, 11 years later, DP told me I had to unravel everything I'd ever been taught. It was almost like having to learn how to walk for a second time. At times my shots found the floor more frequently than the front wall. But despite the short-term struggles I was encouraged to think of the long-term gains. It was crucial that I stuck with the programme. Once I had started down the path there was no turning back. I couldn't find myself lost in no-man's-land, clutching onto my old style of play and not fully committing to the new style. After each training day I'd get back to DP's at 6pm and collapse on the sofa, totally exhausted by the mental rather than the physical effort involved.

Remember I was competing on the PSA tour at the time. At every tournament, as the pressure mounted, I would revert to my old, elbow-into-the-stomach and carrot-up-the-arse style of play. For ages I was in this limbo in between my old style and the new style DP was trying to instil in me. The entire process took two to three years before we reached a stage we were happy with. And it has been a constant work in progress ever since. In my experience, squash technique is something you can only ever be about 90 per cent happy with. In many ways you might say DP and I are still searching for perfection.

Some of my favourite training sessions are those technical sessions with DP. We have spent so many hours on court in Harrogate, often in winter when the courts are freezing and we have to feed £1 coins into the overhead heater. We've had to cope with dodgy bounces on floorboards warped by the leaky roof. But none of this ever spoils my enjoyment of these sessions. I learn so much every time I'm with DP – and not just when we're on court. Some of my most valuable lessons have been sat around the dinner table or courtside, chatting and putting the squash world to rights. DP has always coached me as a human being, not just as a squash player. Anyone who knows this sport can see his stamp on my game but, at the same time, he has always ensured that it's my personality that shines through, not his. Over the past decade he has been a second father to me, shaping the person I am both on and off the court.

As we were going through that revolution in my playing style, I had to trust my new coach without question or reservation. It was one of the most difficult undertakings of my life. The results were never immediate. During those hours retraining all my basic shots, I used to think of myself as the Karate Kid from those 1980s films, spending all day painting Mr Miyagi's fence, and waxing his car, unaware that I was working on my new technique.

Yet I enjoyed the challenge. DP opened my eyes to different ways of playing squash. He changed the technique of my backhand (enormously) and to a lesser extent my forehand and volley. He taught me about footwork, and weight transfer, and deep lunges. I was a fairly tall guy for a squash player but I never used my wingspan effectively. I'd take little steps around the court, moving up and down, really inefficiently, with no grace. DP taught me to combine my shots with my movement into one effective weapon.

Before I signed up with DP I was ranked around 60 in the world. I was on an upward curve, still fresh from the juniors. However, as much as it pained me to admit it, I knew that if I didn't alter my technique I'd hit a brick wall and my ranking would plateau. Perhaps forever. I'd never reach the top of the sport. But 11 years later, with DP's changes on board, I was world No.1.

I can honestly say that, despite the anguish of totally rebuilding my game, I never for a second doubted DP's plan. I suppose my faith in him was unshakeable because of the track record he had with previous players. He'd coached my idol, Peter Nicol, Britain's first world No.1-ranked player and four-time Commonwealth gold medallist. And he'd coached Cassie Jackman to World Championship glory as well as Paul Johnson and Simon Parke to the world's top four. When we first teamed up he said he was confident that, with the raw materials I had, he could take me to the world top 10. The rest, he said, was up to me.

It was around this time that Peter Nicol famously defected from Scotland to England (citing a lack of support from the Scottish governing body). This was big news at the time, even making front-page headlines in a national newspaper. When Peter joined our squads I finally realised what professional squash was all about. The way he'd warm up before training, the way he'd warm down afterwards, the way he prepared every last tiny piece of equipment, the way he knew exactly what he wanted to reap from every training session, his attention to detail. The other guys were also top world-ranked professionals but there was just something different about Peter. He was a level above in everything he did and he carried this amazing aura about him. I was so impressed. Peter explained to me that, just like me, he had never won much as a junior and that DP had totally dismantled his game, too, at a similar age. Peter was in the middle of five straight years as world No.1 so this was about as glowing an endorsement as you could get. If it was good enough for Peter Nicol, it was certainly good enough for me.

All throughout the retraining process, DP kept encouraging me to persevere. He told me I'd never be completely satisfied but that one day it would all click into place. And I'll never forget the moment it did. It was September 2002 and I was doing a solo practice session at Hallamshire. There had, of course, been incremental stages of success along the way (my ranking had risen to the world top 40) but this was the day everything finally became clear in my mind and my body. It was a Eureka moment. (I had another of those moments later in my career, as you'll discover.) Right then I was so happy. I immediately phoned DP and told him excitedly that finally the ball was going consistently in the directions I wanted it to. During that session I felt I could have put a 50-pence piece on the floor and hit it every time. It was the first time I could see my entire squash career mapped out in front of me. And the results followed. By January 2003 I was ranked top 30 in the world and ready to mix it with the big boys.

I went, as usual, to the chiropractor that evening for treatment on my back. It was the last time I ever needed to go. Perhaps that was the day the carrot finally fell out of my arse.

CHAPTER 6

Seven driving tests

In which we see Nick wrestle with a Bermudan motor
scooter, prang a whole street's worth of car wing-mirrors,
have an altercation with an airbag on the Snake Pass, and
almost puke up on the Nürburgring.

Someone once told me that sportsmen make good drivers. It makes
sense. If you can chase down a little ball moving at speed then you
shouldn't have too much trouble coordinating pedals, a gearstick
and a steering wheel. Driving's just another sport.

I, however, am a terrible driver. I know my way round a squash
court much better than the winding back streets of Sheffield. My
wife Esme says I drive like I play squash: physical, fast and with
little subtlety.

But I can safely say I'm not the worst driver on the PSA tour.
As I discovered on my first trip to Cairo in 1999, there are dozens
of Egyptian players so reckless behind the steering wheel that they
make me look like a professional driving instructor. However, when
it comes to poor car-handling skills, there is one British player who
really does take the biscuit, and that's my good friend Adrian Grant.

Adrian has written off more vehicles than he cares to recall. One
incident I remember in particular was when he was cruising up the
M1 late at night after a league match and felt a bit peckish. He
reached behind him to grab a banana off the back seat just as he sped
over a large puddle in the road. After aquaplaning across the entire
motorway, the car flipped over and ended up a complete write-off.
Adrian and his passenger, Stacey Ross, were lucky to survive.

Another time we were both in the car – he was driving –
heading to Manchester for a national squad training session. We

were climbing up over the Pennines on the Snake Pass, which is treacherous at the best of times, when a car two places ahead of us slowed down to pull over. We ended up shunting the car in front of us. I think Adrian put his foot on the accelerator instead of the brake. The damage was so bad that the horn wouldn't stop sounding for half an hour. The airbags slammed us both so far back into our seats that I had a seatbelt burn mark imprinted across my tracksuit top.

The trouble is we were right at the top of the Snake Pass with no possible mobile phone signal. And we were both slightly hungover from the night before. A breathalyser might have caused a problem or two.

I've had a couple of prangs myself. Once I was driving home from Leeds Bradford airport after a long flight from Cairo. Trying to multi-task – and failing badly – I was texting someone on the phone while driving. (Not clever, I know.) My front wheel struck the kerb, lacerating all the rubber on the tyre. But I soldiered on. I was so exhausted I just wanted to get home and worry about it the following morning. The rim of the wheel must have been scraping on the road because there were sparks flying everywhere and other drivers were flashing their headlights at me. Eventually I pulled over. This homeless bloke happened to be walking past right at that moment. He told me he was on his way from Manchester to Sheffield, on foot. I was fairly new to driving and since I didn't have a clue how to change a tyre, he offered to help. It was a lifesaver. So when he asked me to give him a lift to Sheffield railway station I could hardly refuse. He looked like he'd spent the previous week sleeping in a ditch, and he smelt like it too. As he climbed into my passenger seat I thought there was a serious chance he might slit my throat and steal the car. But he turned out to be a lovely bloke.

The worst car trouble, though, was just a few days after I passed my driving test, in 2004. I'd managed to secure a sponsorship deal which supplied me with a turquoise Mercedes A Class. Not bad for a first car but I shudder to think what the insurance premium must have been. The only snag was that the sponsorship terms meant I had to have my name emblazoned up both sides of the paintwork.

I'd just reached the quarter-finals at the English Open, staged in Sheffield that year, and, along with another player, Joey Barrington (son of the famous Jonah), I decided to go out partying. In that turquoise A Class we must have looked like a couple of hairdressers. But we certainly had no trouble picking up girls.

At the end of the night we offered them a lift home and found ourselves God knows where in Sheffield, at the bottom of this ridiculously steep hill with cars parked tight on either side of the street. The girls asked us to drop them at the base of the hill but, keen to show off, I insisted on taking them to their door. Then I realised there was nowhere to turn the car around. Forced to reverse back down the hill, I clunked the wing mirror of just about every car parked in that street. No doubt a few residents peered out of their front windows to find out what all the commotion was about. There I was in my turquoise car with my name writ large down the side, driving backwards with all the finesse of an Egyptian taxi driver.

Two days later I was at my parents' house when a policeman knocked on the door. One of the residents had complained that I'd done £700 worth of damage to her parked car. I may have been feckless but I knew I'd only scraped the wing mirrors, not the bodywork. And I told that policeman as much. He said: "Son, if the truth is any different to the story you're telling me, I'll be straight back here with the full force of the law!" Fortunately he never came back.

In Bermuda, one year, I had a bit of an altercation with a motor scooter. Again, I was lucky I didn't get in trouble with the police. It was 2004 and there was a group of us on the island for the Bermuda Open. The following day I was due to play Frenchman Thierry Lincou, who had just reached the world No.1 spot for the first time. All the boys had hired scooters so that we could take a look around the island. Of course, I fancied a little ride myself and persuaded Malaysian player Ong Beng Hee to let me go for a burn on his one.

Big mistake. All that I know about scooters you could comfortably write on the inside of a squash ball. Two areas I'm particularly ignorant about are acceleration and braking. So the minute I sat astride Beng Hee's machine, keen to pretend I knew exactly what I was doing, I revved up the engine way too much, slammed it into gear and went skidding horizontally across the main road. I was so lucky there weren't any cars coming. Fortunately the main roads of Bermuda aren't quite as busy as those of the UK.

The scooter ended up trapped on top of me, weighing down on my left ankle, its chrome bits scraping across the tarmac along with my buttocks. When I finally brought my beast under control I had cuts and bruises all the way from my feet up to my lower back. Fortunately they were just flesh wounds and, unbelievably, the next day I beat Lincou in the first round.

***

Given all the bumps and scrapes I've had, you might suspect I had a bit of trouble passing my driving test. And you'd be entirely correct. It wasn't until I was 24 years old that I finally had that coveted document in my hands. I was either a horrendously poor driver or I was jinxed. I like to think it was a combination of the two, and here's why.

My first driving test I failed because I accidentally ended up on a tram track. (Yes, I know it sounds ridiculous.) There are dozens of tram routes criss-crossing the streets of Sheffield and sometimes it can be a bit confusing where the roadway ends and the tramway branches off. Anyway, I was in the wrong place and the test examiner had to yank the steering wheel out of my hands. We weren't facing a head-on collision or anything dramatic like that but he failed me all the same.

At my second driving test I turned up having lost my licence on a trip abroad and they told me to get lost. The third time my test was cancelled because of fog. The fourth time because of snow. (I'm not making this up. Why would I? It's actually quite humiliating.)

The fifth time I passed the test (Wahay!) and then promptly lost my licence again after being caught speeding twice in my first two years. Back to square one.

On my sixth test I was flying through the various procedures when I got pulled up on a technicality. I can't even remember what it was. But I failed. And the driver who was tested just before me – and passed – had had a sign taped to his steering wheel reminding him which way was left and which way was right: that day my humiliation was complete. On the seventh time I finally passed with flying colours.

So I have submitted myself to seven UK driving tests in all.

Where I'm not jinxed, though, is with the cars I get to drive. I'm lucky to be good friends with a bloke called Felix Frixou who runs a car dealership in Duffield, in Derbyshire. For the last 10 years he has supplied me with great sponsorship deals on my cars.

I first met Felix through Duffield Squash Club, for whom I still compete in the national league. It's a great club and, since it's in a village rather than a large town, when the squash team plays everyone comes out to watch. I've played over 10 seasons there now and I love the atmosphere that the squash club generates. On match nights everyone mucks in. Members sell tickets for a raffle, help cook the players' food, run the bar. It's a great old-fashioned sports club. Felix's roles are multifarious. He has been sponsor, manager, coach, bus driver... you name it.

He's a top bloke. A half-Cypriot and half-Scouse car dealer, and a bit of a sporting legend. Although he's now in his 40s, Felix has in the past competed for his native Cyprus in three different sports. He was once goalkeeper for the national football team in a World Cup qualifying match against Italy. He also represented his country in rugby and squash.

The first motor Felix lent me was that hairdresser's turquoise Mercedes that did for all those wing mirrors. Then he offered me a silver Mercedes C Class, again with my name spray-painted down the side. After that it was a VW Touareg.

Fortunately I persuaded Felix to leave my name off the paintwork this time. It was undoubtedly good promotion for both me and his business but it was a tad embarrassing. I couldn't drive badly or resort to road rage because everyone would instantly know who the idiot behind the wheel was.

Luckily for other road-users, my driving skills have improved in recent years. But I've never been much of a car buff. I'm not your typical bloke who appreciates fine cars. In 2010 my manager Paul Walters was promoting the British Grand Prix squash event in Manchester. It was sponsored by motor oil manufacturer Rowe, also owners of a German racing car team. A chap called Michael Zehe from Rowe had arranged a special driving day for me, Paul and Alister Walker at the famous Nürburgring race track. We hit the track in a very powerful Porsche, each getting a turn in the passenger seat while a professional drove. My lap took eight and a half minutes, with a ridiculous top speed of 230mph. I counted as we overtook (and undertook) 30 or so other vehicles, often zipping past with just a couple of centimetres to spare. There are still videos of us up on YouTube. Alister and Paul look like they're having the best day of their lives. I, on the other hand, turn a funny shade of grey and look like I'm about to puke up.

I now play for Michael's Rowe team in Germany's squash Bundesliga but I've never asked him if we can visit the Nürburgring again.

CHAPTER 7

The breakthrough

In which Nick tries to walk five miles across the Sahara Desert, learns about an English bloke called Jim Dear and sympathises with tennis player Andy Murray.

Sixty-seven years without an English winner. The British Open, squash's equivalent of tennis's Wimbledon, hadn't been won by an Englishman since Jim Dear back in 1939. In September 2006 I became the player to finally break that curse. Just as Andy Murray laid the ghost of Fred Perry to rest in 2013, so I did the same for Jim Dear.

As with most successful periods of my career, it all started with a defeat. Less than three weeks earlier I'd arrived at the World Open in Cairo as seventh seed, full of high hopes. Those hopes were quickly dashed after I lost a bad-tempered and highly controversial match to Egyptian Wael El Hindi in the second round. Wael is a good friend of mine but it's fair to say he wasn't always the cleanest player in the world; quite an expert in using his body to block opponents' fair access to the next ball. In fact he made blocking an art form. Very rarely was there a rally that didn't end with an intervention from the referee.

After losing the match to Wael, in a tiebreak in the fifth game, I decided to vent my frustration by walking back to the hotel instead of taking the tournament bus. The only problem was this involved a five-mile trek across the desert... and, apart from the lights of the pyramids, it was pitch black. I got about a third of the way before common sense prevailed. By that time much of my frustration had dissipated.

When you get blocked out of a match as I did on that night, you initially feel like the referee is to blame. You expect him to do more to protect you. There you are trying to play a fair game yet you're the one being punished. It was probably a good idea that I'd hiked off across the desert otherwise I think I might have tried to throttle Wael. Once I'd calmed down, however, and been truly honest with myself, I realised the real reason for my defeat. The truth was I hadn't played well enough. I'd left the ball in the middle of the court, giving Wael lots of chances to block me. If I'd kept the ball glued tightly to the side wall he wouldn't have had so many chances.

Watching my match that night was the legendary former Egyptian player Ahmed Barada. A decent blocker himself, he agreed with my self-criticism. "Fifth game was no good," he said when I bumped into him the following morning at the airport. "You kept hitting the ball in the middle of the court". I thanked him for stating the bleeding obvious and boarded my flight home, tail well and truly between my legs.

The flip side of this early loss was that it gave me a few extra days to regroup and prepare for the British Open in Nottingham just over a week later. It was very unusual to have the two most prestigious events on the PSA tour staged within a couple of weeks of each other. Other competitors – David Palmer, for example, who won that World Open in Cairo, saving five match balls against Gregory Gaultier in the final – were bound to be feeling the pressure of the tour schedule more than I was. I was well rested in comparison.

During that week in between the World Open and the British Open my manager Paul Walters had organised an eight-man exhibition event (the Gerrard Grand Prix), with two pools of four players playing round robin matches before progressing to the finals. For me it was perfect preparation for the British Open. Since no ranking points were available I'm sure some of the players had turned up simply for the appearance fee, but I was determined to make the most of it. Wins over James Willstrop, Amr Shabana and Karim Darwish – plus the honour of actually taking the title – gave me a much needed confidence boost. I was back on track and ready for the British Open.

Much readier than even I had suspected. A few days later I'd reached the British Open final, up against Thierry Lincou. Top seed Amr Shabana had been eliminated from my half of the draw and

I'd fought past James Willstrop in the quarter-finals after he'd been forced to withdraw during the match, still suffering the after-effects of food poisoning from the week before in Cairo. Only Karim Darwish in the semi-finals had tested me. I was fresh, unlike my opponent Thierry who'd had to overcome Lee Beachill, Gregory Gaultier and David Palmer in his half of the draw.

One factor against me, however, just like Andy Murray at Wimbledon, was the weight of history. Everyone kept reminding me this was my moment. The name Jim Dear and the date 1939 were on everyone's lips. Here was my chance to make sporting history.

I needed to block all of this out of my mind, though. I was ranked below Thierry. Yes, I'd been in the world top 10 for a couple of years, reaching the odd semi-final and one major final in Hong Kong, but I was a long way from being a consistent title contender. Thierry, on the other hand, had been World Champion in 2004 and world No.1 for that entire year. Yet I was being cast in the role of favourite. My plan had been to start the match with the feeling that I had nothing to lose but, instead, all this pressure had been heaped onto my shoulders.

My morning practice session was terrible and all I wanted to do was get back to my hotel room for some much needed shut-eye. I knew I might never get a chance like this in the British Open ever again. But I was nervous. Probably the most nervous I've ever been in my entire career. When the match started these nerves were obvious. I could feel that Thierry was a little heavy-legged from his semi-final against David Palmer the night before but I wasn't able to capitalise on that. My squash was frantic and inaccurate, while he was using all his experience. He was slowing the pace, hanging in each rally, giving me no free points at all.

That evening, my manager Paul (who was also tournament promoter) had offered free standing tickets to all members of my home club Hallamshire or my national league team, Duffield, just down the road from Nottingham in Derby. The tournament venue, the University of Nottingham, was packed, everyone supporting me. British fans can often be more reserved in their applause than fans from other countries. They of course get behind the home player but they tend to applaud good squash rather than showing any overt patriotism. On this occasion things were very different.

They were loud, boisterous and determined to give me the lift I so obviously needed. Especially at 4-1 down in the fifth game. By now Thierry was exhausted, yet I still couldn't get the advantage over him. I was still so nervous that I wasn't moving my feet properly. I felt totally flat-footed.

My solution? I told myself to move my feet more. To this day it is probably the simplest piece of advice I have ever told myself during the course of a match. When you're nervous, simple ideas are just what you need. So I began to take shorter steps to reach each ball. I took three when only two were necessary; five when I needed only four.

Suddenly I found I had a spring in my step and this enabled me to prey on Thierry's fatigue. I blasted through the last few points in a blur, raised my hands to the roof and celebrated becoming British Open champion. At once I became aware of the history of the situation: I had won the oldest and most famous trophy in our sport – the first Englishman to do so in 67 years. Jonah Barrington had won it six times (as an Irishman) and Peter Nicol twice (but he was born in Scotland). Seeing my own name on the trophy felt surreal. There I was, alongside luminaries of the sport such as Jahangir and Jansher Khan, players I'd watched and been inspired by at Wembley all those years ago.

The British Open is often referred to as the Wimbledon of squash, and I guess my win was much like Andy Murray's Wimbledon triumph in 2013. His victory came 77 years after the last British winner Fred Perry's. How Andy coped with being reminded of that every year he played is beyond me. The media coverage in tennis far outweighs that in squash. I know for a fact that the news reports of my British Open win were minuscule compared to Andy's after Wimbledon. Not to mention the prize money.

Almost immediately after this huge breakthrough, I then suffered my worst spell on the tour for a number of years. Looking back, I think I felt I'd reached the top of the sport and therefore rested on my laurels for a while. I assumed that because I was British Open champion I would automatically command respect from other players and naturally progress to the top of the world rankings. I thought I had some sort of divine right to win more tournaments and play well on every occasion. The problem was that the other players were more desperate than ever to knock me off my pedestal. Suddenly, a win against me wasn't victory over Nick Matthew but rather victory over the British Open champion.

A few early losses jolted me out of my complacency. But getting my form back wasn't easy – I didn't win another major event until just over a year later, at the US Open in October 2007. It's strange (and more than a little frustrating) that over the course of my career there seems to be a recurring theme where I respond better to failure than to success. After a bad loss I feel the hunger levels inside me rise enormously. I feel the bit between my teeth. It makes me get up extra early in the mornings and do those killer training sessions. It's not that I don't train incredibly hard even when things are going well. It's just that complacency is always nearby, lurking at my doorstep. I seem to take my good form for granted even just to a tiny degree. In a weird sort of way, being out of form keeps me on my toes.

This complacency is a definite weakness of mine, one I've never entirely been able to resolve. Despite that poor form after my first British Open triumph, I learnt a huge amount about my game. It was the first time I properly learned how to handle winning. The whole process took well over a year but without this breakthrough, and the loss of form in its aftermath, I would never have achieved the consistency I found later in my career.

CHAPTER 8

Wounded lion

In which our hero goes under the knife, gets bathed by his mum and wins his first post-operation tournament.

"Ten, nine, eight…zzzzzzzzzzzzzzz"

Anyone who's ever experienced general anaesthetic will recognise this scenario. There you are, lying on the bed, nervous as hell about going under the knife. The anaesthetist injects you full of barbiturates – or whatever drugs they use – and asks you to count backwards from ten. You never make it past eight. Then you're in a coma.

It was January 11th 2008. I was out for the count on the hospital bed having keyhole surgery on a ligament tear in my right shoulder. The surgeon managed to install some sort of high-tech elastic band in there, assuring me it was 100 times stronger than any ligament in the human body. He bunged in some screws for good measure, too, which dissolved away three months later.

I ummed and aahed for ages about whether to have a shoulder operation. As a professional sportsperson, if your body starts to let you down – as it often does – you face a dilemma. Do you soldier on bravely through the pain, hoping treatment and rehab will do the trick, or do you risk an operation with a long recovery period and no guarantee that you'll perform any better afterwards?

My problem was I could no longer soldier on through the pain. It was 2007 when I realised an operation was my only option. I was playing James Willstrop in the final of the English Open in Sheffield – just hitting an ordinary backhand drive was excruciating. I was lucky the tournament was at the English Institute of Sport where I trained daily and had my own physio on site, otherwise there was no way I could have made it even past the first round. I then took two weeks off over Christmas to recover. Despite daily physio treatment I could feel the shoulder was only getting worse. Something desperately needed to change.

I had been diagnosed with something called a SLAP lesion (a superior labral tear from anterior to posterior). I can tell you it was a veritable pain in the posterior. It turns out that the daily grind of playing professional squash had opened up a tear an inch long where my biceps tendon met my shoulder... and if I didn't do anything about it, it was only going to get longer. I had a decision to make – probably the biggest of my career. I could soldier on in pain, not risking an operation. But where would that leave me? I wouldn't exactly be able to play at my best. In the end the worry of a potential drop in ranking was outweighed by the desire to play squash free of pain. Difficult as it was, I took the decision I felt was the best for the long term. I opted for the knife.

Which is how, multiple doctors' appointments later, I found myself lying on a bed in Sheffield's Claremont Hospital counting backwards from ten.

I remember leaving the hospital afterwards in that post-barbiturate glow you get as you're coming down off the anaesthetic. As I walked out of the doors, my arm in a sling, some random guy came up to me and immediately quipped: "Well, it looks like you won't be playing squash for a while." I didn't know him from Adam and quite frankly I was surprised he knew who I was. Having just gone under the knife, I was feeling a little bit sorry for myself. It was nice to be recognised so I nodded away as he started telling me about the glory days of squash in the 1970s; how he had watched Jonah Barrington and Geoff Hunt slug it out on the world's first glass-backed court in the British Open at Abbeydale.

After a few minutes he looked at me quizzically and asked: "Have you ever played squash yourself?" It turned out he hadn't recognised me at all. The quip about me not being able to play squash for a while was sheer coincidence.

Although he was quite right. My surgeon had promised I'd be out of action for only three months. "Not too bad," I thought. "I'll be back on court and training hard in 12 weeks." How wrong I was. What he had meant was that, in three months, I could start using very light weights.

The English Institute of Sport gym in Sheffield became my rehab centre. The first exercise I was allowed to do involved picking up a one-kg dumbbell with my right arm and doing a bicep curl. I then had to take the dumbbell with my left hand before lowering my right arm. I repeated this ten times. How humiliating that was. There I was in a gym full of world-class athletes doing half bicep curls with a one-kg weight. There were grannies lifting more than I was. It was five months before I was able to hit a squash ball in anger and a total of eight months before I was competing again.

They were the longest eight months of my life. Normally I struggle to sit still for a whole movie, let alone spend all day sitting on the sofa. Imagine my frustration, then, at not being able to play the sport I so love. I think I went a bit mental during those eight months.

One of my first distractions was a DVD of the surgeon's chopping job on me that the hospital had presented me with as a parting gift. I managed to watch it for about ten seconds before feeling violently sick and reaching for the remote control. My mum, who's even more squeamish than me, nearly fainted. What they thought I could learn from that DVD I will never know.

Temporarily disabled, I moved back to my parents' house for a couple of months. My dad used to call me "the wounded lion". He was so used to seeing me bounding around the house trying to let off energy but instead I was sitting on the sofa licking my wounds. I could use my legs and left arm but my right arm was completely incapacitated. My mum even had to help me take a bath – not the most dignified experience when you're 27 years old.

All that forced inertia made me incredibly moody. Writing, cooking, washing, driving… I needed help from my mum and dad with all of life's basic tasks which made me feel like a teenager again. A stroppy one at that. I was so frustrated I found myself snapping at my dad if he put my sling on the wrong way, or berating my mum for cooking my porridge incorrectly. I couldn't have been much fun to live with.

Because of the pain in my shoulder, I couldn't even run until five months into my recuperation. However, two days after my operation I started riding a stationary bike, working my core muscles and doing single-leg squats. To this day I find that single-leg squat the most torturous exercise of all because I did so many of them during that recovery period. At the time, my physical trainer Mark Campbell was contracted to me for just two sessions a week but he was kind enough (if that's the correct term to describe any session handed out by Mark) to give me seven or eight. I was nowhere near ready to go on court so I found myself in the gym two or three times a day. Anything to take my mind off the recovering shoulder. We developed a close bond during that period which has remained ever since. I developed a close bond with my arm sling, too. With all the squats and stationary bike rides it got incredibly sweaty and stinky.

There was actually a plus side to those eight months of tedious recuperation and inactivity. I know it sounds like an enormous cliché and, of course, I would much rather have been playing, but it totally reinforced my love of the sport and made me realise just how lucky I was to play squash for a living. I've always responded better to setbacks than to successes so, in many ways, my shoulder operation was a blessing in disguise. It made me more determined than ever to get super-fit, to win tournaments and to climb the world rankings. Without a doubt, if I hadn't suffered that shoulder injury I would never have become the player I've since become. Granted, it stopped me doing my job for eight months, but at the same time it gave me the opportunity to step back from the very insular world of squash and re-examine what I was doing. During those eight months I worked exhaustively on both the physical and mental sides of my game. I watched hundreds of hours of videos of me and my contemporaries competing. There were so many psychological ups and downs during my recuperation that I think it toughened me up mentally more than anything else ever before. Through those experiences I learnt so much about my game, my mindset and squash in general.

There was also a lighter side to my time out from the game. While my shoulder was recovering my dad and I used to challenge each other to racketball at least once a week: best of three games with me playing with my left hand. It was great fun and got me back into the court-specific footwork again. It had the added bonus of being great bonding time between my dad and me. I never did beat him though.

Post-operation, my first tournament back was the Dutch Open in September 2008. Incredibly, I won it. The week before I had been so disillusioned after yet another breakdown in my training that, in desperation, I had phoned my dad. I was at the very end of my tether. In my mind my career was finished. Maybe I was being over-dramatic but I had even started looking for coaching jobs in America. So imagine how delighted I was to win my first tournament back. That week in Holland is still, to this day, one of my most emotional moments in squash. To go through the turmoil of the previous eight months, at times thinking my career was over, and to come out on top made me feel incredibly proud.

However, it was only a medium-tier event. I reached the semi-finals of my next event, the French Open, in Paris but suffered a battering at the hands of Gregory Gaultier, who was now up to No.2 in the world. Before going under the knife I had reached as high as No.5, but once I found myself back in the mix with these top 10 guys I quickly realised just how rusty those months on the sofa had made me. The physical training I had done meant I was comfortably in the best shape of my life. As a touring professional it's rare you get eight straight months to physically strengthen like that. However, it took time to get back into the sport, and to relearn those on-court subtleties that are so crucial during big matches.

During the rest of 2008 I dropped out of the world's top 10. I wasn't playing badly, it was just the lack of ranking points catching up with me. It wasn't until the Tournament of Champions, in New York in January 2009, that I finally started to make my mark again. Much of it was thanks to a lucky break. I was seeded outside the top eight and had a really tough draw with the Aussie Stewart Boswell in the first round followed by world No.1 Amr Shabana in the last 16. Stewart injured his back the day before our match, so I enjoyed a first-round walkover. Then Amr pulled out after a game and a half. In the quarter-finals I beat James Willstrop, who I could see was suffering with a heavy cold, and in the semis I got past Ramy Ashour. Eventually my luck ran out and I lost to Gregory Gaultier in the final. My confidence was back, however. I was champing at the bit.

My comeback continued with wins in Sweden and at the National Championships in February. I suppose I was lucky in that

I benefitted from quite a few walkovers during that period. Even the Swedish Open final gave me a walkover against Karim Darwish, who had injured his ankle in his semi-final. Players started joking that my new shoulder was jinxing other players and causing them to drop out of matches. I wasn't complaining, though. After eight months out I needed a bit of luck on my side. By the end of 2009 I had won the Qatar Classic and reached No.2 in the world.

CHAPTER 9

2,000 matches and counting

In which Nick applies surgical spirit to a blister (Ow!), signs a female fan's chest, has his match interrupted by a kidney transplant and enjoys the world's fieriest chicken wings.

In my life I've completed more than 2,000 squash matches. After all these years it's impossible to be exact but it's got to be somewhere around that figure: 1,000 as a junior and 1,000 as a professional. As much as I love doing what I do, on some days it feels more like 10,000 matches.

In the early days I'd grab my kitbag and, despite my previous coach Mark Hornby's protestations, do a few stretches and walk straight on court. Nowadays, each match requires a meticulous preparation procedure that I would say borders on the obsessive. Actually it's so far beyond obsessive that it's something else entirely. I've talked to many of the other pros and discovered they put themselves through a similar rigmarole.

Preparation starts the minute I get up. Those first few seconds of the day can be disorientating. I've stayed in so many hotels in so many cities that I often wake up with a slight sense of panic. Where the hell am I? Who am I playing today? What stage of the tournament have I reached?

These days, most of the tournaments I'm competing in are at PSA World Series or PSA International level. We're normally put up in decent hotels, four-star standard or above. So the rooms are often comfortable and the breakfasts usually tasty.

As soon as I've fuelled up – always a large bowl of porridge and berries if they're available – I think about my morning practice. Most matches are scheduled for late afternoons or evenings, when maximum spectator numbers can be guaranteed. This frees up our mornings for practice sessions. These are usually with another player, or with my coach if he has been able to travel to the event with me. Occasionally I might do solo practices. I won't work too hard during those morning sessions – 45 minutes maximum – trying to find a nice balance between getting my eye in and conserving energy for the evening match. I have research to do, as well, swotting up on that day's opponent by watching video footage of his matches.

I then consider my match tactics and formulate a game plan. There are three basic elements to every game plan: first off I give myself a confidence boost by reminding myself what my strengths are. I'm physically one of the strongest players in the world; mentally, on a good day, I'm as tough as an MI5 spy under interrogation; and I'm the best volleyer in professional squash. (You have to big yourself up, otherwise what's the point?)

Next up I analyse how I'm going to win the match. What weaknesses does my opponent have that I can exploit? Maybe I'll win more points attacking deep on the backhand? Perhaps I should volley as much as possible? Should I play at fast pace or more subtly with deception?

Finally, I think about my opponent's strengths. I need to block them in any areas where they are really strong. If it's Amr Shabana I'm up against, for example, I know I mustn't put the ball shoulder-height on his forehand or he's likely to kill it. Watch out for Ramy Ashour's backhand cross-court volley nick. Don't give James Willstrop too many angles for his infamous drop shots from the back of the court. Never get in a backhand battle with Gregory Gaultier at the front of the court because he's the best in the world at that. Karim Darwish has the best forehand front deception in the game. I look at my opponents as a menagerie of lethal animals, all of which have special weapons I need to be wary of. One's a tiger with razor-sharp teeth and claws. Another's a scorpion with a sting in his tail. Spitting cobras, stinging jellyfish, venomous biting snakes, charging rhinos… each player has adapted to deadly effect in a certain area of the game.

During the match I use my three-point game plan to stay one step ahead of my rival. But it's crucial to have a plan B, just in case. Nothing too complicated, just a simple get-out-of-jail card in case things start to go a bit pear-shaped. Maybe I'll just focus on hitting the back wall with my length shots. Perhaps I'll concentrate on getting the ball past their volley, or moving my feet faster, or dominating the T. This plan B will help me overcome any nerves since I'll be focusing on a tactic change that's small and manageable, and it will hopefully change the momentum of the match to my advantage.

After my practice session, buoyed by a good, solid game plan, I return to the hotel to chill out until it's match time. There's clothing and equipment to organise, of course. Most important are my rackets. When I was younger I'd travel with just two or three, making use of the tournament stringer whenever I broke a string. But different stringers have different stringing styles. You never get two rackets precisely the same which, at our level of squash, can be really off-putting. Even just a pound per square inch too tight or too loose and it can affect my whole game. At a Milan tournament, once, the stringer strung my racket so tightly that on just the first shot of the warm-up it cracked and the head split open. When I came back to my seat the racket looked more like a bow and arrow than something you were supposed to play squash with. For that reason, nowadays, I leave home with at least six rackets, all strung to perfection and ready for battle.

It's my dad who's in charge of restrings. A day or two before I fly out to a tournament he prepares all the rackets for me. I use a fairly durable Ashaway string at around 27lbs which is quite low compared to most of the other pros. Some go as high as 32lbs but I find the lower tension helps me control the ball better. I can get enough power at this tension but, at the same time, I get a good feel for my drop shots at the front of the court.

My dad has a high-tech, modern and, most important of all, exceedingly accurate stringing machine. He keeps it at the club shop in Hallamshire where he now works. Back in the mid-2000s, he and I had an agreement that I would buy the stringing machine for him as an investment and in return he would give me free restrings up to ten times the retail value of the machine. Since the machine cost £1,500 and he's given me around 10,000 restrings at £10 labour each time, I reckon I've done fairly well out of the deal. It's about time he started charging me but, until now, I've kept schtum.

I am fastidious about the way I put on my racket grips. I've spent years painstakingly perfecting the technique for this. For training I don't mind what colour grips I use but for tournaments it has to be yellow. They feel the best to me. At a push I can just about deal with the blue ones. But, psychologically, yellow grips put me in good stead for the match. Yellow means business.

The colours yellow and blue have become a sort of signature for me. My shoes, my racket, sometimes my match kit, all feature those two colours. My website and all the marketing material for my squash academy in Sheffield share it too.

Initially it wasn't a conscious decision. I was at a photo shoot years ago for Dunlop shortly after I signed a racket deal with them. At that stage I wasn't important enough to request what colour my rackets should be sprayed. The racket they had me pose with for the photos was a fairly dull white and silver. "This is hardly going to set the world on fire," I thought. The Dunlop rep had another model, a beginner's racket sprayed up in blue and yellow. It looked far more dynamic in the photos so I asked him if I could switch over. The next day the company supplied me with my own line of rackets in the same colours. I've stuck with that colour scheme ever since.

Rackets ready, I then change into my match kit and place my racket bag on the hotel bed. (This is important, as you'll discover in the next chapter.) I always have three or four identical shirts for each match. It's rare that I don't sweat through the lot of them. Now that our matches are broadcast on Squash TV, the shirts must be identical. We're not allowed to switch colours in the middle of a match since it can confuse the TV audience. There's now a whole protocol where you have to tell the tournament organisers in advance what colour shirt you plan to compete in. The higher-ranked player gets to choose first, while the lower-ranked player has to ensure he's in a different colour. One of the many benefits Squash TV has brought to the game is a greater range of shirt colours. In the old days you'd often see the two players both in traditional white. TV and the need to instantly distinguish both players has encouraged clothing sponsors to be more adventurous in their designs, too. Alister Walker, who rarely steps out in anything but bold fluorescents, is perhaps the most adventurous of all.

I always turn up for a match with two pairs of shoes just in case

I need to change halfway through – long matches can be brutal on the feet. Ideally, both pairs will be worn in and match ready. On my weeks off I'm always wearing brand new pairs around the house to gradually wear them in. It takes two to three weeks of house wear to get them perfectly match-ready, so I have this constant conveyor belt, moulding brand-new shoes to the shape of my feet. The last thing I need is blisters. Short of breaking a limb, blisters are one of the worst injuries a squash player can suffer from because of the gruesome agony they cause. In the wrong place, a blister just the size of a pea can be the difference between triumph and disaster. It's bizarre to think that a whole tournament campaign can hinge on a tiny piece of skin.

I used to get horrendous blisters on the balls of my feet when I was younger before I switched to Hi-Tec shoes. I remember the physios occasionally cutting off a piece of skin the size and shape of a Pringle crisp. Then they'd apply surgical spirit to the raw skin beneath. The pain lasts just three seconds but is so intense it makes you grit your teeth and clench your buttocks like your life depends on it. I still maintain that those little three-second surgical spirit applications have been the most unbearable moments of my life.

The blisters got so bad that eventually I had to be fitted for insoles. In my early 20s I went to Northwich Park Hospital, in London, to see a specialist. Nowadays I get sent a dozen pairs a year through the post, each one lasting a month. They're basic blister-prevention insoles – nothing too complicated. I once tried your all-singing, all-dancing custom-made orthotics (at around £150 a pair) but they made my knees hurt. I prefer to let my feet react as naturally as possible with the court surface. High-tech podiatric orthotics can overcompensate too much and prevent your feet from really feeling the court beneath you. They're not for me.

Even with insoles, I still have to pay great attention to my feet. One of my worst experiences was in 2010 when I beat James Willstrop at Canary Wharf. The following day I could barely walk. Every time I put my foot on the floor it felt like I was treading on broken glass. They felt more like claws than feet. I had to have an hour's foot massage before I could even stand up properly.

Often I tape up the big toe of my right foot before a match. As many as seven out of 10 lunges can be on my dominant right side, so that right big toe takes a mighty hammering. Because I play forehands with an open stance (right foot forward) and backhands mostly with a closed stance (right foot also forward), on some days it can be as much as 90 per cent of lunges onto my right foot. Imagine the pressure.

Once all the rest of my vital match equipment is stowed in my bag – towels, shorts, socks, sweatbands, iPod, balls, grips, skipping rope, energy gels, energy bars, electrolyte drinks, exercise bands – it's time to leave the hotel for the tournament venue. Most events supply official cars or buses but occasionally you are left to your own devices. At the Hong Kong Open you jump in a taxi. At the Tournament of Champions, which is held in New York City's Grand Central Terminal, the hotel is so close that all the players walk.

My aim is always to arrive just before the match prior to mine. I don't want to get there too early and find myself hanging around for ages. At the same time I don't want to arrive late and in a panic. I need time for my warm-up. Plus, it's good to watch the players on before me so as to gauge how the court is playing that particular day. The same squash court can feel radically different depending on the temperature, the humidity, the air pressure, the time of day, the number of spectators in the venue. All these factors influence how the ball bounces. It sounds pernickety but at our level of squash we need to be prepared for the slightest change in conditions. That's why scouting the court beforehand is so crucial.

On a warm, humid court the ball plays fast like a racketball, bouncing waist high off the back wall, running through much quicker than usual. It feels bigger and heavier on your racket and much harder to control. With a bouncier ball like that you need to play much more patiently, conserving energy by not chasing the ball around.

On a colder, drier court the ball feels more dead, like a stone, especially on glass walls which don't rebound as quickly as concrete walls. You have to strike the ball harder and follow through more. To get yourself out of pressure situations you need to use the full height of the court. Glass courts tend to feel much bigger than traditional club courts as the ball sticks to the glass longer before the rebound. It's only a few nanoseconds but it can feel like an age. It's bizarre what a difference it makes. It gives the impression that the court has an extra foot of space both front and back. These conditions often suit my game since I like to set up base around the middle of the court and cut out shots with volleys.

Overall I prefer a balance: a court that's relatively dead with its bounces but not too cold. Too warm and bouncy, and I can't play my aggressive volley game. Too cold and it benefits the likes of shotmakers like Ramy Ashour or James Willstrop. Somewhere in between the two suits me best. I also love a nice high roof so I can chuck in lots of lobs. The glass-backed court they've named after me at Hallamshire is one of the highest I've ever played on, almost twice as high as some of those on the PSA tour.

Forty minutes before I'm due on court, I start my pre-match warm-up. There's a bit of guesswork involved since the match before me might last 30 minutes, it might last two hours. With my iPod playing some upbeat tunes (Jay-Z, Kanye West, Swedish House Mafia, David Guetta, that kind of stuff) I do a bit of jogging, a bit of skipping, some ghosting movements, lunging, plyometrics, ankle hops, footwork drills and upper body exercises, especially on my right shoulder – the one that was operated on back in 2008. If we're lucky, the tournament might supply a gym for us to warm up in. At most events we have just a small room or even a simple tent. At New York's Tournament of Champions, space in Grand Central Terminal is at a bit of a premium so we have to warm up under the stands. If you need a longer jog then you have to take on the busy commuters on the station concourse. Often you can be warming up in the same space as your opponent, which makes things a little tricky.

All throughout this warm-up I'll have one eye on the current match. You don't want to start your warm-up too late and fail to be properly prepared. In Qatar in 2007 I left my contact lenses in my hotel room and, after rushing back to get them, I had to start my warm-up in the car. There's barely room to swing a cat on the back seat, let alone a skipping rope.

At the same time, it's a mistake to warm up too early in case you peak too soon and run out of energy during the actual match. Semi-finals are notoriously difficult to gauge because they go out live from Squash TV to broadcasters all around the world. These channels can't risk dead air on live TV so one semi-final must run seamlessly into the next. Mistime your warm-up and it's tough luck. At the British Grand Prix in Manchester in 2012 I was on court after the Gregory Gaultier vs James Willstrop clash which went to five games, one of them reaching 20-18. It felt like I was warming up for an hour and a half, and I started to tire. About 15 times I had to stop halfway through and start all over again.

If you've ever been to a PSA tournament you'll know that each player is introduced by the compere. At the Canary Wharf Classic or the North American Open it's an affable English chap called Alan Thatcher. In Manchester it's usually Andrew Nickeas. In New York we have the soothing tones of Don Goodwin. In the Middle East it tends to be the Welshman Robert Edwards. Robert has been on the tour since the days of Jahangir and Jansher Khan and is the expert at hyping up a match. I call him the Marmite compere: some players and spectators love his introductions while others can't wait for him to shut up and let the squash start. I'm in the former category. When I won the 2010 World Open in Saudi Arabia, so intense was the build-up to the final, my eyes were literally popping out of my head before I came on court. In my opinion, Robert is an expert at getting the crowd buzzing.

Occasionally the comperes are required to carry out tasks well above and beyond the call of duty. One bizarre incident that will always stick in my mind was during the 2012 Canary Wharf Classic. I was just about to serve in the middle of my first-round match when, suddenly, Alan Thatcher's voice rang out over the sound system. He wanted to locate one of the spectators rather urgently. It turns out this particular spectator (who had turned off his mobile phone so as not to disturb play) needed a new kidney. The transplant team at his hospital had telephoned the tournament to tell him an organ was available and that he should hotfoot it across town as quickly as his existing kidney would allow him to.

I bumped into this chap at the same tournament the following year where he and his new kidney seemed to be getting along famously. He even apologised to me for interrupting my match the year before.

The tournament comperes love to refer to us players by our nicknames. Many of these monikers were originally coined by the main Squash TV commentator Joey Barrington in an effort to reintroduce to squash some of the gladiatorial features the sport enjoyed during his father Jonah's heyday in the 1960s and 1970s. Like in darts or snooker, some of them are a bit cheesy: Ramy Ashour is the Artist, James Willstrop is the Marksman, Amr Shabana the Maestro, Gregory Gaultier is Asterix, Karim Darwish the Dark Prince, Alister Walker the Predator, I'm the Wolf. But there's no doubt they add an extra element to the sport. It's a great way for the audience to connect with a player's style and, more importantly, personality. I actually quite like my nickname. I've been called a lot worse than the Wolf in my time, believe me. My favourite nicknames of all are Omar Mosaad's, whom Joey has christened the Hammer of Thor thanks to his hard-hitting style, and Simon Rosner's, who is the German Tree-Chopper. He really does swing from so high on his forehand, and so steeply, that you can imagine him with a lumberjack outfit on.

Once the compere has introduced each player, now comes the obligatory handshake with one's opponent. I always ensure I smile and look as relaxed as possible at this stage, even if I'm trembling inside. It's crucial your opponent thinks you're super-confident, looking forward to battle. Back in 2003, in Qatar, I reached the semi-finals and was due to have my match broadcast on the Sky Sports highlight package for the first time. (Back then you only made it onto TV if you reached the semi-finals.) I was understandably quite nervous. My opponent Lee Beachill could see it plainly on my face. Afterwards he told another player that I looked as white as a sheet as we shook hands. Before the match had even started he knew victory was his. Ever since that day I've always hidden any nerves behind a poker face. When I beat Gregory Gaultier in the World Open final in 2011 I could tell he was incredibly nervous as we shook hands. So nervous, in fact, that it looked to me as if he had tears in his eyes. He might have been suffering from some other ailment but seeing those tears gave me the boost I needed. Especially when I was very nervous myself.

Once the match starts, that's when we really start to earn our bucks. This is what we live for. This is when we push ourselves to the physical and mental limits. Game on.

I tend to over-analyse stuff while I'm playing a match. There are often way too many ideas buzzing about my brain – worrying about my shot selection, worrying about my tactics, worrying what position my opponent is in, worrying about technique, getting frustrated by the referee. I know it's always better if I keep things simple, though. Remember my three-point game plan? As much as possible I try to focus on that.

The two times I won the Worlds, in 2010 and 2011, I managed to concentrate on my game plan throughout. All I thought about were the processes of playing squash, not the eventual outcome. I forced myself not to, even for a split second, imagine myself holding up the trophy. So both times, when I eventually won the match, it felt like a surprise. Like I'd just inadvertently stumbled across the finish line of a marathon without realising it. That's how to keep the game plan simple. It gives you more space in your brain to focus on the task at hand.

Saying that, it's very rare that matches go totally according to plan. I can think of only four in my entire career: the Commonwealth Games final against James Willstrop in 2010, the semi-final of the 2010 World Open against Amr Shabana, the semi-final of the 2012 Tournament of Champions against Gregory Gaultier, and the 2012 British Open final against Ramy Ashour. (More about those matches later.)

On the PSA tour we're given just two minutes' rest in between games. How you spend these precious moments is crucial. I head off the court to my chair where I listen to DP's advice. If DP's not at the tournament it will be either my best friend Neil Guirey or Chris Robertson (England national coach) in my corner. Half of my two minutes has passed before they can get a word in edgeways as I'm often so pumped up from the game I've just played that I talk directly at them, answering my own questions. Then they tell me to shut up while they give me their money's worth of advice. It's important they offer only one or two key points; any more can confuse the issue. I use these few seconds to change my sweaty shirt and take on board some fluid.

All players have to rehydrate in between games. There's a fine balance between drinking too little (and later dehydrating) and drinking too much (where liquid is sloshing about in your stomach). I tend to edge towards the latter. Better to have too much on board than not enough. The other players laugh at how pedantic I am with my fluid intake. I'm never seen without a bottle of water in my hand. And I guzzle it down at a rate of knots. The Olympic rower Matthew Pinsent certainly noticed this when he was working as a BBC journalist at the Commonwealth Games in Delhi. In his report he wrote: "Just seen Nick Matthew arrive for his men's squash final with no fewer than seven bottles of water and sports drink with him. He is obviously in no doubt as to how hard the match is going to be." Seven bottles. I told you I was beyond obsessive.

I sweat a lot, so I mustn't fail to hydrate, but I'm by no means one of the heavier sweaters on the tour. Just imagine how hot it gets inside a tournament squash court, especially in some of the warmer destinations on the PSA tour such as South America, Asia or the Middle East. I've been in jungles less humid than some of the courts we compete on. Certain players come off after just one game and it looks like they've been in the shower. This explains why we wipe our palms on the court wall in between points and why court moppers have to regularly wipe the sweat off the floor. I wish I could wear a headband round my forehead like some players do. The trouble is it makes my head feel like it's in a vice. I'd rather have a nice loose forehead, even if the sweat is flying off it like a sprinkler.

By now the two minutes is up so I do a quick quad stretch and circle of the arms (more of my OCD habits) and I'm ready for the next game.

Work doesn't finish when the match finishes. After autograph requests (these range from the mundane to the ridiculous – I once got asked to sign a woman's bare cleavage, like the film character Happy Gilmore) I do a warm-down that involves five minutes on a stationary bike or jogging, just to flush out the lactic acid. Throughout this I'll be slurping on a recovery drink with protein in it. The second you come off court after a match win you have to start preparing for the following day. This first 30 minutes is crucial: you have to begin refuelling so that your body can start repairing itself. Bear in mind it will normally be less than 24 hours until your next match.

Next I see the physio (hopefully Jade is at the tournament), who will check me over for war wounds and often give me a quick massage. I don't actually stretch my muscles until I get back to my hotel. Stretch too early and you can aggravate tiny tears inside the muscles. These tears need a bit of time to knit back together.

Then there are radio and press interviews – TV if we're lucky. I'm always happy to talk to the press. At most of the major tournaments there will be representatives from websites, the odd newspaper and the odd specialist squash magazine. It's nothing like football where even a league match has a press room crammed with dozens of national newspaper sports writers. Our press room often doubles up as a player lounge. At most you'll have a handful of squash writers in attendance.

There are some great characters plying their trade on the PSA tour. Some of my favourites include Framboise Gommendy (who famously calls us players her "babies"), Ian McKenzie (great laugh but don't get stuck on the phone with him or you'll be there all day), Rod Gilmour (Ex-Telegraph but with such a nose for a story that I joke he should have worked for the tabloid press), Martin Bronstein (top bloke except for the time he described me as a journeyman when I was only 23 years old. He was probably right, though) and Richard Eaton (great guy and the consummate professional writer).

Finally, we can head back to the hotel. If it was an evening match, which, to attract more spectators, it often is for us top players, then by this stage it could be well after midnight. I've got to eat, though, and that may require some persuasive cajoling in the hotel kitchen. I've just burned over 1,000 calories on the squash court so going to bed without dinner is unthinkable. The contents of the mini-bar simply aren't good enough. You try refuelling with M&Ms and a Toblerone.

At most tournaments players are allocated two to a room. My roommate may have had an afternoon match, in which case he will be in La La Land while I'm still buzzing on adrenalin from my match. I find it impossible to sleep until my mind and body have properly wound down. With my roommate snoring away I can hardly put on my favourite action movie. I've spent many a late night sitting with my laptop in the hotel lobby waiting for the adrenalin to subside. I'd much rather go to bed at 2am, fully relaxed, than lie in bed at midnight, still wired from the match I've just played. Quality of sleep is more important than length of sleep.

I remember playing at an Egyptian tournament one year where I roomed with Adrian Grant. All his matches were scheduled for the afternoons, all mine for the evenings. Inevitably, I'd come back to the hotel to find him fast asleep. After two nights of lying bolt upright in bed, listening to him snore, I quickly realised I was much better off chilling out in the hotel reception for a couple of hours until sleep arrived naturally.

Squash fans are often surprised to learn that the players have to share hotel rooms. Most weeks I'm really happy to have a roommate. Away from home, for weeks on end, the PSA tour can be a lonely place. Get on with your roomie and you have someone to chat to, someone to share dinner with, someone to go out on the town with (should you both lose), someone to discuss with you the finer points of your game. It helps if he's not your opponent in the next match.

On my first year on the PSA tour I flew out to the Hong Kong Open with Adrian, both of us in qualifying, both in the same hotel room. After we'd each brushed aside a local player we then found ourselves facing each other in the draw. Slightly uncomfortable, to say the least, since we'd been hanging out and practising together all week. The morning of our match, in an effort to make things feel vaguely natural, we decided to travel separately to the tournament venue. I won the match 3-2. It wasn't much fun when we got back to our room. He was very annoyed and I could hardly gloat about my win.

Other weeks I find a roommate irritating. He might be a vigorous snorer, or farter (that's usually me) or worse. Sometimes I really need my own space, in which case I can always pay a supplement to the hotel for a single room. Or DP might be at the tournament with me, in which case we'll often share a room to save money. (Earplugs are essential when DP's in town.) Occasionally I'm lucky enough to have my wife Esme travel out with me. Rest assured, there's never any hanky panky the night before a match. I'm there strictly on business which means my mind must be exclusively on my squash.

After 15 years on the tour, all the hotels tend to blur into one. Some stand out for the oddest reasons, though. At the Renaissance Harbour View, in Hong Kong, I know that if you fail to hang the 'Do Not Disturb' sign on your door, you will, without fail, get woken at 7am by the chambermaid. (Not always a bad thing since the breakfasts are the best on tour.)

The Sheraton, in Boston, has the best spicy chicken wings. One year, sharing dinner with Lee Beachill, we ordered a baker's dozen of them. The 13th got left on the plate as both our mouths were on fire.

The Grand Hyatt, in New York City, connects directly with Grand Central Terminal so you can walk straight from the lobby to the courts without stepping outside. Ideal since it's January and often minus 20 degrees outside.

At the hotel in the Pakistan city of Peshawar, ordering room service is often a game of Russian Roulette. Survive the first day without erupting from both ends and you stick with that choice of food for the rest of the week. For breakfast, lunch *and* dinner.

On the other end of the food scale is the Grand Regency, in Doha, where I assure you the penne arrabbiata is the best you'll find anywhere on the planet outside of Italy.

The most amazing hotel bar I've ever come across is the St Giles Hotel, in New York City. It's so cool and trendy I once saw them filming an episode of Keeping Up with the Kardashians there. The swankiest hotel on the tour, with chandeliers, Doric columns, grand staircases and architectural features that would put interior designer Laurence Llewelyn-Bowen to shame, is the Jefferson, in Richmond, Virginia. The Steigenberger Golf Resort, in the Egyptian resort of El Gouna, has the best hotel golf course I've ever played on. It's never a total disaster to lose early at that event.

Isn't it bizarre? I can describe in detail the minutiae of the hotels we stay in but I generally haven't a clue about the people, the sights, the architecture or the culture of the countries we visit. That's the nature of professional sport. You fly into a city, you head straight for the hotel, you practise, you compete, you eat, you sleep. Then the following days you do it all over again until you lose, pack your bags, head for the airport and fly home.

This is a routine I'm desperate to change. I'm approaching my mid-30s now. It's obvious I don't have a great deal of time left on the tour. Some of these places I will never again get to visit, which makes me all the more keen to see them as a tourist rather than as a visiting sportsman.

One area I've tried to immerse myself in while touring the world is local cuisine. I suppose I fancy myself as a bit of a foodie. Yet because of the risk of food poisoning we rarely push the boat out. I never eat shellfish, for example. One dodgy prawn could make the difference between dying in the first round and hoisting the trophy above my shoulders. And I never chance it with street food. Not since I got pole-axed with food poisoning one year in Hong Kong, courtesy of an unhygienic street vendor.

The oppressive routine of the tournaments means we rarely have time to discover some of the more unusual restaurants in the cities we visit. In New York, for example, we finish competing so late at night that we rarely eat more than three or four blocks away from the hotel. Before the event starts we try to seek out more adventurous places to eat. I'm told that in that city you can find a restaurant representing virtually every nation on the planet. I haven't even scratched the surface of all the amazing culinary delights on offer.

At exhibition matches you can let your hair down a lot more. A few times a year I'm really lucky to be invited to exhibition tournaments at various luxury venues around the world. They wine you, they dine you, they put you up in lovely hotels, and in return you have to play a friendly squash match. It makes us feel like kids in sweet shops. We can enjoy a few drinks the night before a match without worrying that it will affect our performance. We can visit local tourist sights. We can hang out with people who don't spend their entire lives eating, drinking, breathing squash. And at the same time we are bringing publicity to a squash venue. It's great for us, great for the venue and great for the spectators.

I hope to do a lot of these exhibition events after I retire from professional squash. Perhaps I can make up for all those cities I competed in but never properly experienced. I can't wait.

Not all exhibitions go swimmingly, though, as I discovered in 2011 when I almost killed my opponent on the court. It was at Berkhamsted Squash Club, in Hertfordshire, and I was due to play Daryl Selby with the money raised going to a brain tumour charity. As a warm-up to the main event I played a friendly with Simon Scott, from squash racket manufacturer Harrow. Apparently he'd made a handsome donation to the charity for the opportunity to take me on. I didn't want to disappoint Simon (or the large crowd that had turned up to watch) so I decided to give him a proper run-around.

Simon is actually quite a strong player and he was determined to chase down every shot I hit. But halfway through the second game he uncharacteristically let a drop shot go. I turned round to see him bent over double. Thinking he was just tired, I called to the crowd to give him some encouragement. He slowly sank lower and lower until eventually he was laid flat on his back on the floor with a blank stare on his face, white as a sheet. I panicked and yelled for someone to call an ambulance. I really thought I'd killed him.

Luckily there was a doctor among the spectators who leapt into action. He placed Simon in the recovery position and tended to him while the ambulance arrived. It turned out he'd suffered a seizure. When the medics carried him away on a stretcher, he seemed incredibly calm. I half expected him to ask what the score was and request that we continue playing. By that stage I felt like I was the one who needed an ambulance. It transpired that Simon had had a brain tumour as a child (hence his support for the charity) and occasionally suffered from seizures. Fortunately he made a full recovery.

Ironically, just before my match with Simon had started, the event organiser had told me to play without mercy and "run him into the ground". Talk about taking advice literally.

CHAPTER 10

Bag on the bed

In which Nick explains his shoelace-tying ritual, his mental trick for having a siesta and his jewellery thieving alongside Ramy Ashour.

I have an inexplicable penchant for Yakult yoghurt drinks. Open my fridge any time of the week and you'll find dozens and dozens of these little yoghurt bottles staring out at you. Look a bit closer and you'll spot something unusual about them – all the labels are facing towards you.

Yes, I know it's slightly scary but I line up all my Yakult bottles so the labels are facing the same way. I do exactly the same with the other drinks and sauces in the fridge. And much to Esme's annoyance, the vitamins in the bathroom cabinet, too.

It's not the only obsessive-compulsive habit I have. Whenever I put on a pair of shoes I always lace up the left one first. Without exception. I have no idea why I need to do this – it just feels right. And you should see my racket bag. It's like a metaphor for my mind. In the right-hand pocket are all my rackets, lined up perfectly with yellow grips and all the Dunlop stencils on the strings facing the same way. Then, in the left-hand pocket of my racket bag, are my two pairs of squash shoes and my skipping rope. Both the left and right-hand pockets are immaculately clean and tidy.

In the middle pocket, however, it's total and utter chaos. It's like that drawer that everyone has in their kitchen – a repository for all the rubbish that doesn't have a home anywhere else. Perhaps you've seen that episode of the American sitcom Friends where OCD Monica has a cupboard with all her mess in it? Well, I call the middle pocket of my racket bag "Monica's cupboard": energy gels, energy bars, electrolyte drinks, exercise bands, notes about other players on the tour, training programmes, towels, shorts, socks, about half a million sweatbands and my iPod. It seems like my whole life is in that pocket. Maybe the tidy bag-pockets are how I would like my mind to operate while that chaotic middle pocket is how my mind really is.

Get me at a tournament and my obsessive-compulsive habits go into overdrive. Many players have pre-match rituals – always using the same shower, eating the same meal, staying in the same hotel room – but mine really take the biscuit. Here's an example: I once arrived at a tournament hotel and immediately unpacked my suitcase and put all my clothes in the hotel wardrobe. That week I played like a zombie, losing early against a player I should have demolished. So what have I done since that experience? Now, whichever hotel I'm staying at, even if it has Louis XIV chests of drawers and Queen Anne wardrobes (antiques aren't my strong point, by the way), I still insist on leaving my clothes unpacked in my cases. Just because of the memory of that one tournament where I unpacked and lost. Crazy, isn't it?

If I choose a brand of drinking water at the start of a tournament and then compete well in my opening match, I'll force myself to stick loyally to that brand of water for the remainder of the tournament. Even if they're offering another brand for free, I'll go out of my way to find a supermarket that stocks my new favourite water. I'd even take a taxi ride across the other side of town to find it. Psychologically, it's that important to me. Esme says I remind her of that crazy Nicolas Cage character in the film Matchstick Men. I hope I'm not that bad. He's agoraphobic, mysophobic, OCD and he yells "Pygmies!" whenever something upsets him. Fortunately I haven't reached that stage yet.

OCD is actually fairly commonplace amongst top sportsmen. David Beckham has admitted that he has to straighten all the furniture in his house, and that when he puts packets of food in his fridge they must be stored in an even number; if there's an odd number he'll throw away the offending item. Steven Gerrard is apparently an obsessive hand washer. Tennis player Rafa Nadal is a pretty serious OCD case, too. Have you ever seen the way he lines up his water bottles perfectly in between games, avoids stepping on the court lines and, most bizarrely of all, pulls his underpants from between the cheeks of his buttocks before he serves?

Squash player Saurav Ghosal is even worse. I once shared a hotel room with him at the North American Open. The way he lines his rackets and shoes up against the wall makes my habits look like child's play. Next time you watch Saurav play, notice that he won't come off court at the end of each game until he has hit a forehand drop shot that he's happy with. I once told Wael El Hindi this and Wael decided to pocket the ball after the warm-up. With no ritual drop shot to hit, Saurav was in pieces and promptly lost the first game of the match before regrouping.

You'd think that, given the endless hours that we professional sportsmen spend honing our skills, we should be confident in our ability to execute them under pressure. Yet so many of us feel the need to rely on these irrelevant idiosyncrasies to make us feel more comfortable. One player I used to train with, just like Nadal, refused to walk on the red court lines in between points. Yet he must have stepped on them a million times during rallies. In the 2013 World Team Championships I noticed that the South African player Clinton Leeuw appeared to have this habit of using his finger to write (what he hoped would be) his next points tally on the wall before each rally. So, the game score might be 4-4. He would mark out the number 5 with his finger on the wall, hoping he'd win the following point to reach 5-4. Was this positive thinking or OCD overload? When does such behaviour cease to be a comfort and actually become detrimental to your game?

In the past I've done a lot of sports psychology work with a chap called Dr Mark Bawden who works at the English Institute of Sport. One of my problems was I was finding it really difficult to relax in between matches. I'd come off court after a particularly tense contest and I'd be both physically and mentally knackered. Yet I just couldn't switch off from match mode. I'd be lying down on my hotel bed and my brain would be whirring as if I was still on court in the heat of the battle. It was infuriating, not to mention exhausting. I needed a psychological trick to get me out of match mode and into relaxation mode.

Mark's idea was simple but ingenious. He told me to come up with a cue that would persuade my mind to switch off; to stop thinking about the match I'd just played and to unwind. It all came to a head at the Qatar Classic in 2009. I was staying at the Grand Regency in Doha and I'd been allocated a room facing the hotel lobby. There was no daylight coming into my room so I would wake up not knowing whether it was midday or midnight. It was really monkeying around with my body clock. That was when I devised my psychological cue for switching off. It sounds pretty obvious but it worked perfectly. I simply undressed out of all my match kit and put on my normal clothes or my pyjamas instead. I'd then be in relaxation or sleep mode.

The only problem was I also needed a psychological cue to get my mind back into match mode the following day. For some reason, simply changing back into my match kit wasn't working. I needed a stronger cue.

Eventually I came up with the idea of placing my racket bag on my hotel bed. This was just the ploy I needed. I would see my Dunlop bag sitting all alone on top of the duvet and it was like a trigger had gone off in my head. Suddenly I was ready to get into match mode, ready to compete, ready to take on the world.

These psychological cues need to be really clear-cut. There is so much down time at tournaments that it's impossible to be on high alert all of the time. A tournament might last eight days yet you only need to get yourself in that special match mode once a day, for at best a couple of hours. You need to be able to conserve energy yet raise your energy levels, almost at will, whenever you need to. My failure to do all this was probably one of the reasons why in the early part of my career I reached semi-finals or finals but didn't have the mental stamina to go all the way. It's a skill that's mightily tough to perfect.

Quite often when I'm on tour I will have a siesta in the afternoon. Perhaps I'll be practising in the morning and playing in the evening. To keep my body in tip-top condition I will often need an extra bit of sleep. An afternoon siesta is perfect. But, as everyone knows, it's not easy dropping off to sleep in the middle of the day. Sleep now comes easy, however, thanks to my psychological cue. I just put on my pyjamas, lie down on the bed and within minutes I'm snoring away. I'll set the alarm for between 45 minutes and an hour later. The second I wake up I then place my racket bag on the bed. Almost immediately I'm wide awake and raring to go.

Mark has transformed my mental game. Sometimes I feel like he has climbed inside my head and, like a mechanic, repaired all the stuff that didn't work properly.

I've been working with him since I was 25. Back then I was ranked between No.5 and No.8 in the world, capable of beating the top guys on occasions but never consistent enough to challenge for the top spot. Mark and I delved into some amazing psychology during that period. I remember getting to the final of the English Open in Sheffield, in 2005, after working hard with Mark on ways to handle playing in front of your home crowd. In Sheffield, in previous years, I had always tried too hard to impress. I was too worried about what all my friends and family were thinking of me. Mark taught me to "control the controllables", as he said, and not to worry about things that were out of my control. The only problem with our sessions was that they were too reactive. I would go to a tournament and come back with a psychological problem, hoping that Mark could fix it. If I had a habit of blowing big leads I would come back home and we would work on that during our next session. We weren't being proactive enough, however. And that's one of the reasons why my shoulder injury, in 2008, was such a blessing in disguise. With no tournaments distracting us, it gave us time to examine every single aspect of my game: tactics, technique, fitness, power, discipline. Mark talked at length with my coach, DP, and trainer, Mark Campbell. He gave them these charts on which they would give me marks out of 10 in different areas such as speed, flexibility, power, backhand technique, concentration; any area I needed to be strong in. The bottom line was that I didn't really have any weaknesses. It sounds conceited but I was strong in every area of squash: technically effective, tactically clever, fast around the court, powerful, fit as a butcher's dog. So why was I plateauing at No.5 in the world instead of gunning for the top of the rankings?

Mark taught me that to be one of the world's very best you need to have lots of winning weapons. And if they're just very good weapons, that's not enough. What you need is an excellent weapon, or a "super strength", as we called it. My problem was that I was good but I was eight out of 10 at all of these different areas. I didn't have a single area where I was 10 out of 10.

We analysed top athletes from other sports. Tiger Woods, for example. He wasn't the best driver off the tee but mentally he was way above his peers and no one putted better than him under pressure. We looked at how David Beckham was, at the time, without doubt the greatest right-footed set-piece kicker in the world. He wasn't the fastest player or the best header of the ball but he didn't need to be. Give him the ball on the right wing and he would deliver with pinpoint accuracy every single time. Rafael Nadal had, far and away, the most astounding topspin forehand tennis had ever seen. Ricky Ponting was the planet's king of the pull shot. All these greats had one thing in common: they excelled in one particular area.

Mark and I then looked at my squash player peers in the world top 10. Every one of them possessed his own world-beating skill. As I've stated previously, Amr Shabana had an invincible forehand volley. With Ramy Ashour you could never give him a ball at shoulder-height on the backhand because he'd take you out with a cross-court nick. Gregory Gaultier was the world's master at low shots. Karim Darwish had the best forehand deception in the entire sport. James Willstrop had a better touch game than anyone else. David Palmer was by far the most physically and mentally tough guy on the tour.

But what did I have? I had no single skill that really made me stand out. Yes, I was good at volleying and I was extremely fit. But I wasn't the best volleyer in the world, nor was I the fittest player in the world. There was my answer. Mark told me to come back and see him when I was the world's best at both those skills.

A couple of years later, after I'd recovered from my shoulder operation, I think I can safely say that I was the fittest player in the world. I also practised my volleying so assiduously that I became the best technician in the world at that particular shot. I'd done it. Even better than that: I had two world-beating skills in my armoury. I had turned my strengths into super-strengths, into match-winning weapons. Now my opponents all had two things they needed to worry about whenever they were playing me.

Yet my mental game still needed some serious work. I was a bit like Wayne Rooney – psychologically inconsistent. Rooney wouldn't be the astounding player he is without that extraordinary passion and emotion he has but sometimes he sails dangerously close to the wind. At any minute there's a risk his passion might overflow into temper with a rash tackle or violent reaction that earns him a red card. During that period of my career I was often equally rash on the court. Yet I wanted to become the world's top squash player. To do that I needed to be psychologically consistent over the whole season.

I believe every human being has a devil on one shoulder, whispering evil thoughts into their ear, and an angel on the other, whispering good thoughts. When it comes to the battle of professional sport, the volume of those whispers is turned up so loud it sometimes sounds like shouting. During a match you just don't have time to make a measured decision. It has to be instant. That means your thinking processes have to be totally clear under pressure, never clouded by the adrenalin. The problems come when the devil's shouting is louder than the angel's.

Mark made me read a book called The Inner Game of Tennis by W. Timothy Gallwey, which helped me better understand the inner workings of my mind. All of us put so much pressure on ourselves to perform, whether it's a simple day-to-day task, or it's playing sport at the highest level. This can lead to massive amounts of frustration when we don't perform as well as we would like to. We are all very rarely in full control of our emotions. Mark and I came up with this clever way of countering this; a way of measuring my mental state. I imagined a rev counter on a car, with a rising scale of one to five. When my matches needed me to give more fire, more energy, I would crank up the rev counter.

At one on the counter I was passive, emotionless – The Robot. I was cruising along, playing on auto-pilot, with no intensity or game plan.

At two I was icy, cool, clinical and calm – The Assassin. I was the cold-hearted killer, able to pick off my prey without emotion.

At three I was totally disciplined and playing with controlled aggression – The Warrior.

At four I was The Wolf, my Squash TV nickname. This was a bit like when you use your power boost in a video game. You can't use it all the time or you risk getting exhausted so, instead, you save it for crucial moments such as when your opponent's on the ropes and you want to finish him off, or when you're in big trouble and need to counter-attack.

At five I was swinging wildly at the ball, red-faced, angry, with no consistent strategy – The Thug.

In previous years I had spent too many of my matches fighting at level three or four – The Warrior or The Wolf. During the 2009 British Open, for example, I played 100 per cent The Wolf, probably edging into The Thug mode at times, and that simply wasn't sustainable. In the long run it would drain too much mental energy out of me. To win tournaments month in, month out, I needed to rein things back a bit and spend more time at level two, in assassin mode. That didn't necessarily agree with my natural personality, which is much more fiery than that. But Mark knew that if I wanted to get to the top of the world I needed to be cooler, and mentally more economical in my matches. Before he had tinkered with my brain I was playing 80 per cent The Warrior or The Wolf, and 20 per cent The Assassin. Where I actually needed to be was 70 per cent The Assassin, 20 per cent The Warrior and then, at the end of each match, 10 per cent The Wolf. My mantra became "Fire in the belly, ice in the mind".

This all sounds great on paper, but how did it work in practice? At first I made some mistakes. At the 2009 Petrosport Open in Cairo I was drawn against Aussie player Cameron Pilley. Trying out my new psychological attitude, I failed to display any emotion whatsoever during the match and got soundly beaten. On other occasions I have certainly slipped back into the old bad habits. Most obvious are the times I get overly frustrated with the referees. The mental game is much like the technical game in that you are always striving for perfection yet often far from it.

Anyone who has followed my career will know that I am one of the toughest players to beat in the sport. I've never had a problem maintaining this toughness. I would rather roll over and die than be beaten, and I'm happy to sweat blood for my cause. (Hence the title of this book.) I detest losing and, if I'm totally honest, have rarely been a noble loser. I think this is a good thing in some ways. If you aren't disappointed, or hurting, when you lose, you clearly don't want victory badly enough. I once read a quotation which said: "Show me a good loser and I will show you a loser". This rings true to me in many ways but it is perhaps a tad harsh. There are many great champions who I'm sure hate losing with a passion but are still gracious in defeat. Roger Federer and Rafa Nadal spring to mind. In squash Daryl Selby is a great example. I sometimes wonder how he reacts so positively in the minutes following a loss. When Daryl beat me in the final of the British Nationals in 2011 (I was strong favourite to win) the hothead inside me wanted to smash my racket into a thousand pieces but I managed to take a leaf out of his book and be totally dignified in defeat. It was very difficult, though. My old coach Mark Hornby used to advise me to remain humble in both victory and defeat, and it's a lesson we could all do well to remember, even when we're under the most intense pressure.

Overall I am still prone to those petulant outbursts. I long for consistent composure and mental fortitude in my game. I still get the odd bad day at the office, I still fall out occasionally with opponents and I still talk back too much to referees. But my mental game has improved beyond recognition in the past four or five years.

Against some players you can concentrate as much as humanly possible on your own psychological power but never even get a look-in. Ramy Ashour is a perfect case in point. He is brutal in the way he pushes you to your mental limits. It almost feels like he's poking you in the ribs while you're trying to play a shot. Yet the second you turn round he's nowhere to be seen.

Ramy and I are so different in our mental playing styles. It sounds strange but I always say that if we happened to team up as jewellery thieves, Ramy would escape with all the jewels whereas I'd get caught by the police with my hand through the jeweller's shop window. I'm the heavy-footed Yorkshireman while he's the sly, subtle Egyptian. Even if he were to get caught, he has this charmingly innocent smile that makes you forgive anything naughty he might have done. I, on the other hand, often need to have the last word. And too often I imagine that last word is the correct one.

Over the years of playing Ramy, he has successfully wound me up so many times. He often makes me see red mist. It's so frustrating. You are always treading a tightrope between the aggression needed to hurt him and the composure needed to beat him.

We have been rivals for the top spot in the world rankings over the past few years, and we're two totally different characters. So it's not entirely surprising we haven't always got on swimmingly. When you play against somebody with whom you don't always see eye to eye, it's important you don't make the match a personal vendetta. You have to stay professional at all times. I have maintained this well with James Willstrop over the years but have struggled at times against Ramy. Maybe it's the extra physical pressure he puts me under. Or the pace he plays at, not to mention the incredible shots he hits. It can all leave my thought processes heavily frayed at times.

For a long time after the World Team Championships final in 2010, I held a grudge against Ramy. He went two games up in that match yet I managed to reach game ball in the third game. Then he hit a shot which was clearly down. Everyone saw it except for the referees. In the changing rooms afterwards Ramy pretended he hadn't actually seen the ball despite the fact that, on court, he had sworn it was a good shot. In the following match James Willstrop, who is well known as one of the most honest players on the tour, won a point in identical fashion. When challenged on it by his opponent Karim Darwish, James simply pointed to Ramy and me – by now we were seated in the front row, watching the match – implying that it was an eye for an eye. That's very unlike James but it proves how strongly he felt about the issue. How our entire team felt, in fact.

I really should have left the problem on the court yet it was constantly nagging at me. I just couldn't let it drop. The bad blood between Ramy and me lingered over our next few matches. I was making our contests far too personal and it started affecting my performances. In 2012, after a bad-tempered US Open semi-final against Ramy, I responded instinctively, and appallingly, to a push in the back he gave me by jabbing my elbow back towards him. It was more of a frustrated action than an aggressive act, and fortunately I didn't make contact, but it finally made me realise that enough was enough.

We exchanged a few words on Twitter after that. Ramy accused me of being unprofessional (which on that occasion he was correct about) and I responded by telling him to take a good look in the mirror. We all have our faults – and I was prepared to admit to mine – but I hate it when people assume they are perfect. It was a petty argument based on a petty altercation, although in hindsight it was probably beneficial for me. It certainly got things out in the open, and I've certainly moved on since then. The more recent matches between Ramy and me have been much better spirited. We've still fought with a feisty edge, as you would expect from two of the world's top players, but there's been no funny business. Unfortunately, at the time of writing, the results have still been going Ramy's way but I feel like I'm getting closer all the time. The important thing is we have played the game as it's meant to be played: hard, yet fair. We may not be close friends but we have enormous respect for each other.

Despite our previous problems, the defining match between Ramy and me was a classic for all the right reasons. It was at the Saudi International, four days before Christmas 2009. This was a really big deal. It was the final of the first tournament ever broadcast live on the new internet TV channel, Squash TV. The winner was also guaranteed the world No.1 spot for the first time.

I went into the match with precisely the correct mentality. There were over 1,000 Saudis and Egyptians cheering for Ramy and just three Brits cheering for me. The tournament was in a resort in an area of Saudi called Al Khobar, quite far away from any major city and close to the Bahrain border. It felt like they had shipped in a rented crowd of supporters. None of the spectators seemed to know much about squash – they just lifted the roof off every time Ramy won a point. I didn't get worked up in the slightest, though. I kept thinking about all my supporters back home in Sheffield, in the Hallamshire bar, cheering me on. I remained in my perfect assassin mode, playing calmly yet with purpose throughout. I used warrior mode when I had to but generally kept things cool all the way through. Guttingly, though, I lost 11-8 in the fifth game after two hours of us both playing the best squash we possibly could. Ramy got to world No.1 and I was at No.2. It was so humid on that Arabian court that by the end of the match there was sweat seeping through our socks and shoes onto the court surface. Neither of us could stand up it was so wet.

After that match I admit I became obsessed about beating Ramy. Instead of concentrating on my strengths, I directed all my energy into worrying about his strengths. Mentally, that's not a healthy place to be in. I thought that if I could beat Ramy then I could use the same technique and tactics to beat everyone else. Even when I eventually got to world No.1 I was still obsessing over Ramy. I may have reached the top of the world rankings but for every win I notched over him, he was twice beating me. This was by no means a disgrace since Ramy is on course to be one of the greatest players the sport has ever seen. But for too long he was my nemesis and I couldn't stop thinking about him. I was losing sleep. I had to find a way of taking on Ramy as if he were just another player.

Then came the 2012 British Open. It was staged at the O2 Arena, in London. I delivered the perfect mental performance. On June 20th, up against Ramy in the final, everything I'd been working on over the last few years – especially all the psychological stuff – suddenly clicked into place. I beat Ramy 11-9, 11-4, 11-8 in front of a packed crowd. Everything dovetailed tactically, technically, physically and mentally. It was an absolute career-defining moment, as close to perfection as I think I will ever get.

***

In recent seasons I've worked on my mental game with former rugby league player Ellery Hanley. He may be more accustomed to large oval balls than small spherical ones, but he's a very keen squash player all the same and you'll always find him at the UK's major squash tournaments. He enjoyed a stunning rugby career with 34 caps for Great Britain and an MBE for his services to sport. So he knows full well what kind of psychology is required to compete at the top level.

I first met Ellery at the English Open in 2004 when he took on Scottish and former world No.1 squash player John White in an exhibition match. But it wasn't until more recently that we worked together. When Ellery played for Wigan his team won everything. He would pride himself on being the fittest and mentally strongest player in the sport. (He was once even voted the best rugby league player on the planet.) This is the type of mentality he tries to instil in me. Despite an incredible attention to detail, his advice always seems so clear and simple. For each match he will ask me to focus my attention on one key point. If I'm playing Karim Darwish, for example, he'll remind me to bust a gut to win the point immediately after any really long rally since Karim relies so much on his momentum. If I'm playing James Willstrop, Ellery's mantra is "sustained pressure". When I'm playing well he calls me "the caged animal". He always stresses how, the moment the very best players step on court, they must have "no excuses, win or lose". As a professional, you can only give your absolute best. Even if you subsequently lose, you must learn from that and move on. I have found it truly inspiring to learn so much from someone who was so successful in his own sport.

***

DP has also had some amazing success working on the mental side of my game. While he of course concentrates on technique and tactics, he nevertheless knows his way around the complicated circuitry of a squash player's brain. To this day, one of my biggest weaknesses is that I am prone to getting complacent when I am three points ahead of my opponent. I take my foot off the gas and let the other player make a counter-attack. So I'll be 7-4 up and suddenly let my game drift for a few rallies so that the score gets back to 7-all. All that hard work I've done to get three points up can be undone in the blink of an eye, especially when I'm up against someone like Ramy.

Since I'm a big football fan (I support Sheffield Wednesday for my sins), Mark encouraged me to think about this problem in terms of football. I was playing like England when I should have been more of a Manchester United. When Man Utd are 2-nil up they always go for the third goal. But when England are just 1-nil up they spend the rest of the match defending. Now if I'm ever leading in a match and I feel complacency starting to creep in I give myself a psychological kick up the arse. It might just be a whispered word or two of self-encouragement – "Move your feet!" or "Pick your racket head up!" – but it's enough for me to stop my opponent getting back into the game.

When it comes to motivation, DP and I don't really have conventional methods. He neither dangles the carrot for me, nor wields the stick. To get me truly focused requires something a bit more extreme.

Let me give you an example. In 2003 I was selected for the England team for the first time. DP was national coach. We were at the World Team Championships in Vienna and I made my debut against Hungary in the pool stages but then spent the knockout stages of the tournament with my backside stuck firmly on the reserve bench. I couldn't understand why DP wouldn't pick me. If anything, since he was my personal coach, I thought he might show me favouritism. But he wouldn't give me a chance to prove my mettle.

Halfway through the tournament he took me to one side and said: "Nick, this is a team tournament. We simply can't trust you because your performances have been so up and down."

I was gutted. I moped back to the bench, more determined than ever to prove that I was worthy of team selection but mightily annoyed I was still a humble reserve.

In the quarter-finals we were up against Canada. Peter Nicol had beaten Jonathon Power in an epic match and James Willstrop was playing Shahier Razik in the deciding rubber. Towards the end of his match James got a nasty blow to the calf. He struggled through to victory but it was obvious he wouldn't be right for the semis the next day. Suddenly I found myself called into action. Here was my chance to shine. At the time I was ranked No.28 in the world but, as DP rightly assessed, my performances had been too inconsistent. I was first match on against the French No.3 Jean-Michel Arcucci, who was ranked only a few places below me. On paper it was a fifty-fifty match. Nevertheless I played out of my skin and won 9-2, 9-0, 9-1. It was obvious what was going on inside my head. DP had told me I wasn't good enough to compete at this level, so I wanted to prove him wrong by playing a blinder. As a psychological tactic it worked brilliantly. To this day DP still uses this kind of reverse psychology to drive me to success.

I've always been one of those people who responds positively to setbacks, disappointments, even negative comments. Tell me I can't do something and I will die trying to prove you wrong. To this day I remain convinced that one of the reasons for my success was a throwaway comment that a squash journalist once made to me on an aeroplane flight. It was 2005 and I was on my way from Hong Kong to Islamabad. Sat next to me on the flight was one of the journalists on the squash tour – French woman Framboise Gommendy. I get on really well with Fram but I'm sure she won't mind me saying she can be a little eccentric. I remember our conversation that day vividly.

James Willstrop had just become world No.2 and the top player in Britain. I was ranked well below him at No.10 in the world. At that stage we were on a brutal five-week tour, taking in Qatar, Hong Kong, the World Team Championships in Pakistan, and Saudi Arabia. James had beaten me 3-0 on his way to winning in Qatar and, in Hong Kong, we again found ourselves on court together in the last 16. I was pretty fresh while James was knackered from his exploits the week before. Sure enough, I leapt to a 2-0 lead. I assumed I'd already done enough to win the match when something in my brain went "Pop!" Despite being obviously physically drained, James fought back and beat me 3-2. I couldn't believe it.

After the match, on the flight home, Framboise and I were discussing what had happened. She told me not to beat myself up. "After all, it was James you were playing," she said.

She didn't mean to put me down at all. She was simply pointing out what everyone else thought: James was a better player than me and I shouldn't expect to beat him. My God, though, was I riled by that! I remember thinking "Why does everyone think James is this golden child that I'll never beat? I don't care if it's James Willstrop, Jahangir Khan or Muhammad 'I'm hard' Bruce Lee. He's only human and I'm going to be as good as him, if not better."

So perhaps I have Framboise to thank for pushing me to overtake James. As much as her comment was a throwaway one, it planted a seed in my mind that has kept me strong ever since. I now apply this attitude to all my opponents. I will never lie down to anyone, no matter how good they are. Any time I feel an opponent running ahead of me, all I do is remind myself that he's just another human being.

CHAPTER 11

My Eureka moment

In which we see Nick receiving an award from the
Scouts, getting fined £500 for smashing his racket,
and finally reaching world No.1.

Everyone has a Eureka moment at least once in his life. It's how Albert Einstein worked out the theory of relativity. It's how Isaac Newton explained the apple falling on his head. It's how Archimedes figured out the displacement of water.

Now, far be it for me to place a humble squash player in the same category as those great scientific minds but, in January 2010, I had a wonderful Eureka moment of my own. I was reading an article on a squash website written by a top Egyptian coach in which he stated that Ramy Ashour was guaranteed to be world No.1 for the rest of 2010. I can't tell you how much that got my goat. It was like a gauntlet being thrown down at my feet. Exactly the kind of taunt I needed to spur me on to challenge Ramy. Like I explained in the previous chapter, if you tell me I can't do something, then that makes me try even harder to do that very thing. So, by stating that Ramy would be world No.1 for the rest of the year, that particular Egyptian coach was actually making the job of usurping him easier for me. It was a red rag to a bull.

After reading the article I went for a long run around Sheffield with my trainer Mark Campbell. There's nothing like a hard run to focus your mind – my dad, the PE teacher, taught me that years ago. And with Mark to talk to while I was running, my mind was more focused than ever. We ran for 45 minutes that day and I admit I spent about 44 of those minutes chewing Mark's ear off. (Not easy when you're running hard.) I was properly riled by what the Egyptian coach had said. It wasn't so much the thought of Ramy remaining at No.1 all year; it was simply the arrogance and air of superiority with which this guy had written his comment. I didn't even know who he was. When you play a tournament in Egypt, the Egyptian players often turn up with multiple support-team members the rest of us have never seen before. It's hilarious watching them all trying to squeeze onto the player's bench behind the court. There's one guy to towel the player down, another to change his grip, another to fetch his drink. Then there are a further three or four to give advice on how to play the next game. It may well have been only Ramy's towel guy who wrote the comment about his guaranteed No.1 spot but it riled me all the same, especially as it was headline news on the prominent Squash Site website.

A few days before, I had lost to Ramy in the semi-finals of the Tournament of Champions in New York. I was too often looking for the cheap way out. I wasn't prepared to play the long game like I had done in Saudi Arabia only a few weeks earlier. I wasn't willing to endure two hours of pain and torment only to yet again come out on the losing side. Ramy had played well while I gave a weak mental performance. The result was that Ramy wiped the floor with me.

During my long run round Sheffield with Mark, these losses to Ramy were really weighing on my mind. By the end of the run I had vowed I would never lose another squash match in my life unless I had expended so much physical and mental effort that I had to crawl off the court. I swore to leave my guts, heart and soul on the floor before ever again conceding a match.

It really was my Eureka moment. I don't know what was so special about that run around Sheffield – we were running down Ecclesall Road, a route we had done scores of times before – but over the next six months I would win 35 matches in a row. Seven straight titles. It was the most purple patch of my career so far. I won the Swedish Open, the British National Championships, the North American Open, the Canary Wharf Classic, I was in the England team that won the European Team Championships, and, finally, in May 2010, I won the Sky Squash International in Cairo, topping the world rankings. (I also won the Australian Open title in August, after the summer break.)

Perhaps Ramy had been resting on his laurels. Maybe he never expected anyone to mount a serious challenge. Reaching world No.1 surprised me even more given that, not long before, I'd lost the services of my coach DP.

It all came about as a total bombshell. I'd finished 2009 really strongly, ranked No.2 in the world, and I finally felt the world top spot was within my grasp. But suddenly DP, who had spent the last 15 years as England's national coach, was let go from his role. The decision came totally out of the blue, shocking us both. He was still one of the best squash coaches on the planet. He knew it was perhaps time for someone fresh to take on the role but had assumed the Commonwealth Games in Delhi, later in 2010, would have been the perfect swansong; a fitting reward for having put his life and soul into the job for so many years. That way the next coach to be appointed would then have four years to prepare for the following Commonwealth Games.

In this era of squash the role of national coach is far more than simply giving advice on the court. You have to justify and record every move you make. DP is quite a maverick. He has never once recorded the advice he's given during a coaching session. His style is to teach from the hip, following what he feels in his guts rather than anything it says in a textbook. His technique works incredibly successfully. Perhaps I had taken DP's role for granted. I had grown used to him being around at tournaments, paid to be there by England Squash & Racketball. I wasn't sure I could afford to hire him independently to attend all my tournaments. This isn't tennis, where all the top players surround themselves with a massive support team at every event.

What annoyed me most, however, was that the timing of DP's dismissal was unnecessarily disruptive. Here I was trying to become the best player in the world and I was without the support of a coach. What's more, the England team was preparing for the Commonwealth Games without a leader. DP became increasingly ill in the aftermath of this decision. He had felt disrespected and undermined by the manner in which he was dismissed. In the end, both parties ended up in legal wranglings and DP was off work with stress for months. My head, too, was all over the place. Here was my chance to become the top-ranked player in the world. I couldn't blow it. I wouldn't blow it. I decided I had to turn negative into positive. Over the next few months I made myself compete as much for DP as for myself. That made me a stronger player.

The irony now is that it was the best thing that ever happened to DP. By then he had become bogged down in the politics of his role at England Squash & Racketball. Nowadays, though, he's his own boss. He can coach whom he pleases, when he pleases and he can travel to whichever tournaments he likes. He is like a new man now. It's a shame his relationship with the governing body of squash ended on such a sour note. Under DP's tutelage England had enjoyed their finest era. Yet he left with such a bad taste in the mouth.

Fortunately DP gets on brilliantly with his successor as national coach – the affable Aussie Chris Robertson – but it's such a shame that his unique level of expertise isn't being used by those in charge of the sport. The players of tomorrow won't benefit from the same deep knowledge and insight that I was fortunate to benefit from.

So there I was, competing in the Sky Squash International, the last tournament of the season, without a coach. It was staged at the Sky Executive Resort, an impressive country club, in New Cairo City, to the east of the Egyptian capital, with squash courts, tennis courts, a football pitch, a running track, a gym and a huge swimming pool an acre in size.

Both Ramy and I knew what was at stake. Whoever progressed further than the other in the tournament draw would find himself at the top of the world rankings. I was taking things very seriously. I'm sure Ramy was, too.

With our tournament hotel a 40-minute drive from the club, every morning we'd catch this rickety old bus so we could practise on the courts. During the day the heat was incredible. After practice sessions I'd head back to the hotel, chill out in the air-conditioning all afternoon, and psyche myself up for the evening matches. The club is quite high up in New Cairo, with the wind whipping in from the desert. As a result the glass court was covered with sand and ridiculously slippery. For the first couple of nights it was unplayable.

With me positioned at the bottom of the draw as the No.2 seed, I had been allocated the night shift for most of my matches. Sometimes an anti-social hour like that can really mess with your body clock but that week it didn't affect me in the slightest. I was irked, mind, that the organisers had decided to put me on late every evening. Ramy's matches were scheduled for a much more hospitable hour which made me think they were purposefully trying to put me at a disadvantage. If they were, it had the opposite effect. I was so annoyed with the schedulers that, during the early rounds, I annihilated every one of my opponents in record time. Against Dutchman Laurens Jan Anjema in the second round, for example, I started the match at 11.30pm and by midnight I was on the rickety bus back to the hotel. With my penchant for long, drawn-out matches, this was most unlike me. My manager Paul, who had flown to Cairo in DP's absence, said I was playing like the mighty Jahangir Khan. A massive exaggeration, I know, but I really was at the top of my game. It's the closest I've felt in my whole career to being invincible. Perhaps night-time is when I bring out my best squash.

It also helped that my physio Jade was in Egypt with me. England Squash didn't have the budget to fly her out to the tournament so I offered to pay for her flight instead. My back had been giving me a little gyp the week before and I didn't want to take any risks. Jade, bless her, agreed to take the week off work and come out for a working holiday. It was an amazing gesture and, without it, there's a good chance I wouldn't have made it to world No.1.

In the semi-finals I found myself up against Frenchman Thierry Lincou, always a tough opponent. The first semi-final, between Ramy and Karim Darwish, was on before us. In the breaks between games Paul kept me posted on Ramy, who was gradually letting the match slip away to his compatriot.

I was halfway through my warm-up, trying my best to stay emotionally detached from what was going on. But suddenly I started to feel goose pimples all over my skin. If Ramy lost to Karim and I beat Thierry, the No.1 spot would be mine. This was it. This was my chance to be officially recognised as the best squash player on the planet.

Karim eventually beat Ramy three games to love. I don't know if Ramy was having an off-day or if Karim simply played too well. Truth be told, I didn't really care. I was one match away from fulfilling all my childhood dreams.

But first of all I had to beat Thierry. The nerves and adrenalin were kicking in – possibly too much. The court had sand on it and we were both slipping all over the place. It was a nightmare. But I wasn't in a million years going to let this opportunity pass me by.

The match reached one game all. Thierry had had a much tougher route through the draw, forced to win a brutal five-game match the day before, while I was still relatively fresh. He was a great champion but at a stage in his career where he was perhaps past his best. Of course, he had been in this situation before and knew very well how to crank up the pressure. I was struggling big time. In the third game I somehow scrambled my way to 10-9, game ball up. After a long rally in which he had me scuttling all over the court, Thierry found himself with an absolute sitter to draw level. He smacked it right into the tin, handing me the game 11-9. Remember I was without my coach, though. I had Jade and Paul in my corner but neither are squash coaches. They could encourage me all they liked. What I really needed was some tactical advice that would help me finish Thierry off for good. My game was starting to tighten up, I was so nervous. Much as I tried not to, I found myself over-analysing each point after I'd played it. Paul told me just to hack at the ball and keep it in play. He suggested I let go of my shoulder and hit the ball as hard as possible. There I was, on the verge of becoming the best player in the world, and my game plan was simply to run around the court as fast as I could, stop thinking about my squash, and hit the ball as hard as I could.

Unbelievably, it worked. I won the fourth game 11-5 and I was world No.1 for the first time.

What a kick it was. That evening I fielded what seemed like a thousand phone calls. My phone bill must have been horrendous that month. I was congratulated by everyone I knew, I spoke to sports journalists writing about my success and I replied to countless emails. When I woke up the next morning – remember I still had the final to play – Paul told me to switch off my phone. "You've come here to win the whole tournament, not give up after the semi-finals."

He was right. It wouldn't look good if I reached world No.1 and then failed to try my hardest in the final. But what an incredibly strange feeling. I'd just achieved my lifetime ambition and I still had a match to psyche myself up for the following day. In the final I lost the first game to Karim. I was really enjoying the squash but I wasn't winning enough points. There was no purpose to my play. At the game break I turned to Paul and said, "I'm really loving this. It feels great." He didn't smile. He just said, "You won't be loving it if you lose 3-0."

That was the wake-up call I needed. Complacency had started to creep in because I knew I was world No.1, win or lose. But I would have looked weak if, as world No.1, I'd lost my first match. Paul's words spurred me on and I eventually beat Karim 3-1.

The following day I flew straight home to England and then on to Mexico to meet up with some of my best friends from Sheffield – Mick, Rory, Dave, Sean and Nick – for a week's holiday. I couldn't believe that none of them mentioned the fact that I'd reached world No.1. Had it somehow escaped their attention?

I woke up in my hotel room in the beach resort of Cabo San Lucas, with the Pacific waves lapping outside my window. It was the first of the month, the day the monthly PSA rankings are calculated. I checked on the website to see my name right at the top of the list. That and the view from my window made me a very happy man indeed.

But how on earth had all my friends failed to spot my achievement? Surely one of them had noticed. I was mightily miffed. I thought they might at least have splashed out on a bottle of champagne to celebrate. By dinner time, still no one had mentioned it. I was starting to wonder if I'd become world No.1 at all. Maybe I'd imagined it all.

After dinner, though, I realised it was all a trick. They'd all been pretending they didn't know. Mick and Rory didn't join us for dinner, instead heading off to our favourite local drinking hole, the Nowhere Bar, to organise a special VIP area. That night we partied and drank champagne until the small hours. At one point the barman announced over the PA system what I'd achieved and everyone kept coming up to congratulate me. Hot girls were pulling up my shirt and writing "No.1" in marker pen on my chest. A few of them added their phone number, too. It was my first taste of celebrity status. Well, as close as you can get to it in a sport like squash. And it felt good.

Paul Walters had a special celebration planned for me, too. After the Mexican holiday, with those phone numbers just starting to fade on my chest, I flew back to England for my 30th birthday. I'd hired out Kenwood Hall Hotel in Sheffield and had invited all my friends and family for a big knees-up. Paul wanted to mark my sporting achievement as well as my 30th so he had booked a very smart restaurant – Rowley's in the lovely village of Baslow – the evening before the main party.

It seemed everyone wanted to celebrate with me. Even the local Scout brigade had arranged to come round to my house to give me a special Scout award. Local press were in attendance and I had to pose with the Scouts in my squash kit for the cameras. I was delighted to do it but they turned up an hour late. So there I was, milling about in my squash kit with a photographer from the local newspaper, conscious that I was due to meet Paul and my parents at Rowley's. I figured they wouldn't mind waiting. It was the Scouts, after all.

An hour and a half late, I finally turned up at the restaurant. There were 30 or so people there – friends, family, coaches, physios, trainers, doctors, sponsors, people from England Squash – just about everyone, in fact, who had contributed towards my squash career. And they all wanted to mark my accession to the world No.1 spot. It was a very moving evening. The only problem was I had to blame my late arrival on a group of young Scouts. I suppose it was an original excuse.

***

My winning streak finally ended in August at the Hong Kong Open. I'd won the Australian Open in Canberra just beforehand, which took me up to 33 straight match wins. Not a bad winning streak but just a tad short of Jahangir's record of 555 straight wins in the 1980s. (How on earth was that even possible?) Against Pete Barker in the Hong Kong quarter-finals my luck eventually ran out. This distressed me so much that, on losing to Pete, I smashed my racket full whack into the glass side wall, shattering it to smithereens. Then I walked off court without even picking up the pieces. Not the cleverest thing I've ever done. I hate losing, but this was totally unacceptable behaviour. The PSA immediately hit me with a £500 fine. I was lucky the punishment wasn't more severe. When you're world No.1, and everyone's watching you, it's even more important to set an example.

CHAPTER 12

Blame it on Chris Evans

In which Nick explains his rather volatile relationship
with James Willstrop, James's dad Malcolm and all the
vociferous fans from Pontefract.

It's all Chris Evans's fault. It's thanks to that notorious radio DJ that
my relationship with James Willstrop is so acrimonious.

It all kicked off at the 2009 British Open in Manchester when
James and I found ourselves squaring up to each other in the final.
The media was quite rightly bigging up the match. After all, it was
the first time since the 1930s that there were two Englishmen in the
final. This was quite a deal.

As with all big deals in sport, the media needed to stoke the fire
a bit. And who better to be prodding with a poker than controversial
DJ Chris Evans?

A radio interview with Chris had been arranged for both James
and me simultaneously. It was a bizarre situation. We were sitting
together less than a metre apart in the Manchester HQ of England
Squash, with headphones on, chatting live on Chris's Radio 2 drive
time show barely an hour before the biggest match of our lives.
And Chris was trying to find out just how acrimonious the rivalry
between us really was.

James told him that we got on fine, that we occasionally shared
a hotel room or practised together, but that we didn't exactly share
a dinner table. He explained that we were friendly work colleagues
rather than best mates, which was completely true... at the time.

Then Chris asked if we ever indulged in a bit of cricket-style
sledging on the court. James, probably half seriously and half
jokingly, said: "Yeah, Nick likes to have a word on court from time

to time". And he was correct. I do like to mutter the odd word now and then. I wouldn't exactly call it sledging but I'm sure it can be slightly off-putting for some players. James pretty much admitted this to Chris.

Anyway, fast forward an hour or so and James and I were on court contesting the final. It was a vicious battle, as it often is between us, and after three games James was outplaying me. He was very much on top. The match was slipping away from me and I desperately needed to change the momentum of play in my favour.

There was some really ugly squash coming out of me. I just couldn't control my emotions. I remember arguing with the ref, trying to drum up some sort of animalistic anger inside myself. I was playing flat as a pancake – not surprising when you consider the traumatic week I'd just endured.

Just 72 hours earlier, my infamous back injury (more about that later on) had been so serious and so painful that I'd actually packed my bags in readiness to go home. It was during my second round match against Cameron Pilley that my back degenerated into one of its vicious spasms. These are often so bad that 10 minutes later I'm not even able to tie my shoelaces. On this occasion adrenalin somehow carried me through the match. However, when I woke up the following morning my whole body was so misaligned, so twisted up that, when I tried to stand up straight, my right nipple was a good three or four inches below my left. It turned out I had a bulging disc in my spine that had inflamed massively, causing the rest of my body to contort in compensation. There was no way I could play.

Before my quarter-final against Daryl Selby I had eight hours of physio treatment, passed from one therapist to another, like a lame horse, in a desperate attempt to make it to the court. My plan was just to walk on court, play a couple of rallies, and concede the match to Daryl. That would have been the honourable thing to do. Somehow, though, I managed to complete the entire match. To this day I don't know how on earth I managed it. My back was a ticking time bomb and I kept waiting for it to explode at any point. Knowing that every rally might be my last, I was so tense. Bizarrely, I played better in spite of this physical threat hanging over me. I couldn't move properly so, ironically, the quality of my squash increased dramatically. Instead of competing at a reckless pace – as I'm sometimes wont to do – I kept control of my tempo and accuracy. It was all out of pure desperation but it worked. This was a valuable lesson I would remember for the rest of my career.

After that match against Daryl I was an emotional and physical wreck. Warming down on the outdoor running track outside the tournament venue, I broke down in tears. There were still two more matches to go. There was surely no way my back could hold out that long. Yet somewhere deep down I had this feeling I was now going to win the British Open.

I carried my great form into the semi-final against Peter Barker, beating him too. In many ways that match was even tougher since Pete had been sharing a room with me all week and was intimate with every tiny detail of my back injury.

So there I was in the final, up against James. The atmosphere inside the National Squash Centre was a bear pit, with James's fans from Pontefract on one side of the seating and my fans from Hallamshire on the other. James's dad Malcolm was encouraging his Pontefract boys to make more noise. There was perhaps a bit of squash politics at play here, too. For a while James and I had shared the same manager, Paul Walters, who also happened to be promoter of this tournament. Just a few weeks before the British Open, James had fallen out with Paul and ceased working with him. It seemed as if Malcolm was now desperate for his son not only to win the British Open but also to get one over on Paul in the process. The way the match was going, he was getting his wish. I was going down fast.

Suddenly I remembered our radio interview with Chris Evans and how James had suggested he was vulnerable to a bit of sledging. Chris had planted the seed in my mind that sledging might be an effective extra weapon against James. It wasn't a conscious thing for me but, because the interview had taken place so recently, the idea must have been there at the back of my mind. I perhaps subconsciously knew it was a ploy I could fall back on when things got tough.

Well, it just so happened that the match was getting very tough indeed. At one point James appeared to be intentionally blocking me from reaching certain shots. He is very tall for a squash player – 6ft 4ins – with an incredibly wide wingspan, not to mention his size 13 feet. When you combine this with the fact that my biggest strength is my volleying, it means that accidental collisions around the middle of the court are inevitable. Prior to this match, James had not long recovered from an ankle injury and I thought this might explain why he was slower than usual to clear a path away from the ball. I also thought it might be a deliberate ploy to break up the play. All players, including myself, have been known to do it. It's still exceedingly frustrating, though. I was even more surprised since James's dad (and coach) Malcolm had always banged on about the virtues of fair play. This might explain why, the next time James blocked me from reaching a shot, I turned to him and said without thinking: "Did your dad teach you how to do that?"

I probably said it a bit louder than I should have. I certainly made sure his dad, who was sitting in the front row, could hear it. It was one of those occasions when you think something and, before you know it, you have vocalised it out loud. This kind of thing happens to me a lot. It was hardly what you'd call subtle. But, in one fell swoop, it totally changed the entire course of the match.

It was the emotional kick up the arse I needed, and it put James on the back foot. I hadn't meant him to take the comment personally but it was obvious he had.

It affected him more than I realised. Maybe he made the mistake of thinking about my comment rather than focusing on the match. Up until then he had been right in the zone, moving me around the court like a chess player in charge of his pawn. But suddenly he appeared rattled. The momentum had changed. I clawed back the fourth game to level the match and then we tussled for the deciding fifth. I was so angry in between games that at one point I remember thinking I wanted to rip James's head off. And that's not the kind of emotion that helps in squash. My playing had improved but the emotional rollercoaster I was on wasn't helping me at all. It was all too hit and miss. Soon James was 10-8 up and a point away from victory.

The British Open, as a title, is probably only second to the World Open in terms of prestige. It certainly has more history than any other professional squash event. At the end of your career people always judge you on how many Worlds and how many British

Opens you have won. I had already had my finest moment in squash, winning the British Open in 2006, and here I was a few points away from victory again, three years later. I remember thinking to myself how these opportunities don't come around too often. I might never have another chance. Somehow I managed to rein in my emotion, finally playing with a bit of control. Suddenly my mission became clear. I focused my mind, ridding myself of the demons that had been haunting me for most of the match. James may have been match point up – and I obviously had no margin for error – but I refused to go on the defensive. I decided to attack. I suppose at that point the match was his and I had nothing to lose. I remembered that, in the past, someone had once told me to "play every point like it was match point". So I went high risk, played attacking squash, clawed back the deficit and eventually won the match, and the title, 12-10 in the fifth.

If you need any evidence of how much that tournament meant to both of us, and how emotionally drained we both were at the end, you just need to look at the video clips of those first few moments after my victory. I was flat on my back in the middle of the court, elated, yet totally and utterly spent. James was hiding in the front left corner, his head in his hands. I'm sure he wanted to dig a hole for himself then and there. It was his third defeat in a British Open final (he had lost to Anthony Ricketts in 2005 and had multiple match points in 2008 against David Palmer) and I totally understood just how gutted he must have been.

Bizarrely, the day after that final, there was virtually no coverage of the match on all the usual squash websites. There had been a falling out between the squash media and the promoter (remember that was my manager, Paul) prior to the event. The only proper match report I ever saw was on the website of the British squash magazine Squash Player. Unfortunately, the reporter was none other than Malcolm Willstrop, the dad whom I had, just the day before, sarcastically suggested might have taught James to block his opponents. Malcolm is a superb match analyst and has a track record as a brilliant coach. He is, however, without doubt, the most opinionated person in the entire sport. In his report he slagged me off mercilessly. Anyone who hadn't seen the match would have assumed I was an utter villain. (Granted, I shouldn't have mentioned James's dad on court, but I was hardly a villain. It was a feisty match, that's all.)

Don't get me wrong. I really respect Malcolm Willstrop. He's one of the most successful coaches in the sport and his club, Pontefract Squash & Leisure Club, is a veritable conveyor belt of talent. He has guided the likes of Gawain Briars, Lee Beachill and Vanessa Atkinson to the very top of our sport. Not to mention his own son. All great players.

Of course Malcolm was never going to write a balanced report on a highly emotionally charged match that his son had just lost. There's too much conflict of interest at play. However, from then on the relationship between James and me has been pretty sour, to say the least.

Had James won that 2009 British Open final, I suspect Malcolm would have written a more tempered report and the whole episode would have been forgotten. What happens on court stays on court, to use a cliché.

Only James didn't win. I did. And the whole Pontefract clan went ballistic. Four years on, they are still seething.

***

It's good for any sport to have rivalry. Conflict and antagonism gets people interested. How dull would things be if James and I were best buddies?

Given our enormously differing characters, I suppose it's no surprise we wind each other up. The first time we ever played each other was in a British Championship under-12 match, in Oxford, if I remember correctly. We were in the consolation plate event, having both lost in the first round. I was 11 years old and he was eight. Despite the age gap, he physically towered over me. And he gave me a good spanking. I remember how gutting it was to be beaten by a younger player. When you're 11, an eight-year-old seems like a baby.

After that we often played together on the same Yorkshire junior teams. He was always an age group below me but because he was so talented he got moved up a year. Yet, in individual matches, given our age differences, our paths rarely crossed. It wasn't until we went professional that we found ourselves regularly squaring up on court.

As a junior, he was quite a shy character. Because he was so strong on court he was seen as the golden boy of squash. He won British titles in every age group, taking the World Junior Squash Championships – the ultimate world junior title – in 2002. Everyone rightly assumed he was going to be a great senior champion one day.

I think we've always had a lot of respect for each other. We're totally different characters and we've certainly never been close friends. But, inevitably, in the small, incestuous world that is professional squash, we have spent days, weeks, months (even years, if you add it all up) in each other's company.

I wear my heart on my sleeve, both on the court and off it. I show my passion a lot, and that's something I sometimes have to rein in. James, on the other hand, keeps his emotions in check. I'd describe myself as a very aggressive player. I play at a fast pace, hunting down the ball. I like to intercept shots in the middle of the court, reducing the amount of time my opponent has to react. My real strength is my volley. I love a highly physical game. Thanks to my dad I was a cross-country runner as a kid. This, coupled with the ridiculous pressure sessions Mark Hornby used to put me through, means I love those lung-busting rallies when the sweat starts pouring off. I always thought attacking too early was a sign of weakness. Not for me the subtle touch game at the front of the court. I'd much rather grind my opponent down to a pulp in a ball-breaking 60-shot rally.

James is the complete opposite. He plays with finesse, grace and incredible touch. He can take the pace off the ball at will. He has this amazing skill of making his opponent seem to run three times as far as he does. He delays the ball in the middle of the court and, once his opponent has charged forwards to cover a potentially lethal drop shot, he'll send them deep to the back of the court again, forcing them to do court sprints in the process. Next time the same opponent doesn't push up quite as far, James will play his drop shot and the rally is over. Simple, yet brilliant squash.

Don't get me wrong. He can also grind it out when he needs to. He's an incredibly gutsy player, never accepting defeat, one of the most stubborn competitors I have ever had to take on. In fact, I think this is perhaps his most underrated skill. He is, however, a far more classic-style squash player than I am. His accuracy is so phenomenal that his nickname on Squash TV is the Marksman.

Mine, you'll remember, is the Wolf. I think these two nicknames perfectly sum up our contrasting characteristics as players.

Squash has been described as "physical chess". I'd add a little qualification to that description: "physical chess at 100mph". In which case James is the one playing chess and I'm the one speeding along at 100mph.

Of course, these disparities in character and playing style make for a more intriguing rivalry. Like Bjorn Borg versus John McEnroe. Or Muhammad Ali versus Joe Frazier. Or Seb Coe versus Steve Ovett. I'm the emotional, physical one – the McEnroe, the Ali, the Ovett. James is the cool, calm and controlled one – the Borg, the Frazier, the Coe.

If we hadn't both been so successful then perhaps I'd have no right to mention our rivalry in the same breath as these greats. But both James and I have held the world No.1 spot. For two straight years in 2011 and 2012 we traded the No.1 and No.2 rankings. We have played each other in the finals of World Championships, British Opens, Commonwealth Games and Tournaments of Champions – some of the biggest prizes in our sport.

The fact that we are both Yorkshiremen only stokes up the rivalry even further. My club (Hallamshire) is in South Yorkshire while James's (Pontefract) is in West Yorkshire. I live in Sheffield and he now lives in Harrogate. We may both be Tykes, as Yorkshire people are sometimes known, but technically we're from different counties.

Pontefract Squash & Leisure Club has become internationally famous in the sport. And James's name is now synonymous with the club. Club supporters often follow him to even the most far-flung backwaters of the PSA tour. He might be grinding out an early-round match in Qatar and, suddenly, from the crowd, you'll hear a yell of "Come on Jimbo!" in a broad Yorkshire accent.

My squash club is a wonderful sporting centre but it doesn't have the same tribal loyalty that Pontefract has. So my fans don't travel abroad like James's do. And thanks to the antagonism between James and me, the rivalry between our two clubs is perhaps the strongest out of all the UK's squash clubs.

Matches between the two clubs are always feisty affairs. The club bar at Pontefract directly overlooks the squash courts so that members can prop up the bar while supporting their boys. Occasionally things get a little rowdy.

I'm hardly what you'd call welcome at Pontefract. After that infamous 2009 British Open final, one of the members at Pontefract approached my best friend Neil and told him flatly that I was persona non grata. Not that I ever trained there anyway. Since then, though, I've always felt a bit uncomfortable if I've been forced to play there.

But it seems my popularity at Pontefract is linked directly to my and James's positions in the world rankings. If I'm ranked above him, I'm seen as the evil interloper. When he leapfrogs me in the rankings, however, suddenly I'm an acceptable guest again. In January 2012 I found myself competing in a National League match at Pontefract. I'd been injured for the previous two months and James had won three tournaments in a row and had replaced me at No.1 in the world rankings. As a result, the Pontefractians couldn't have been more welcoming. Their golden boy was No.1 and I was No.2. They saw me as the upstart who had been put firmly back into his subordinate position. As I walked on court for my National League match, Malcolm, who was compere for the evening, took obvious glee in introducing me as "World No.2", with the emphasis on the 2.

I suppose it's like any local derby. Look how hostile relations get when a city has two Premier League football teams. Pontefract and Hallamshire squash clubs are a mere 27 miles apart as the crow flies. And as I was writing this book, one was home to the world No.3, the other to the world No.4. It's bound to be a recipe for serious animosity.

But because James is Malcolm's son and golden boy, that animosity occasionally gets personal. Malcolm can certainly make life difficult for people if he wants to. I'd describe him as a cantankerous cross between Albert Steptoe (from Steptoe and Son) and Brick Top (from the gangster film Snatch). Get on the wrong side of him at your peril. I've got on the wrong side of him several times, simply by beating his son on the squash court or leapfrogging him in the rankings. He dislikes me so much that I've heard stories of him banning juniors from Pontefract for playing with my Dunlop racket. "We don't use that racket here," he has been heard to say. How ridiculous is that?

Amazingly, after that 2009 British Open final, I beat James something like 25 times in a row. That's remarkable for two people who are so closely matched. I know that in each of our clashes, the ill feeling I've had from the Willstrop clan and the Pontefract supporters has had the opposite effect intended and has psychologically helped me beat James. Every time I play him and hear that yell of "Come on Jimbo!" there's something deep in my guts that tells me there's no way I'm going to lose to this guy. The animosity I get from those Pontefract guys is quite unbelievable. Often, even when I'm playing against Frenchman Gregory Gaultier, I hear shouts of "Allez Greg!" in a Pontefract accent.

Not everyone from Pontefract is against me though. One of my most charming memories is of two young lads from the club coming up to me during a junior tournament at Hallamshire. "I hope you don't hate us, Nick," they said. "You are our second favourite player after James. If James isn't playing we always support you." I thought this was a lovely gesture. One of the lads was the son of Mick Todd, James's manager. Mick is sportsmanship personified and always the first to congratulate me after a win against James; or against anyone, for that matter. Malcolm, on the other hand, flatly refuses to even speak to me, never mind congratulate me on a win. He clearly holds a grudge against me which he struggles to let go of. He has even written reviews of three separate tournaments I have won (the 2010 Commonwealth Games, the 2011 World Open and the 2012 British Open) without actually mentioning my name in any of them. It takes some serious journalistic skill to write about a sporting event, to mention the DJ, the compere, even the courtside flower arrangements, but to omit the name of the winner. After all of these years it wouldn't be wise for me to hold my breath, waiting for any sort of congratulation from Malcolm.

***

The highest quality match James and I have ever played has to be the semi-final at the 2010 Canary Wharf Squash Classic. It's very rare to have two top players competing at their very best in the same match. But on that occasion, this was certainly the case. We were throwing the kitchen sink at each other. It was like Rocky Balboa and Apollo Creed.

At one point I found myself losing the third game 20-18 to go 2-1 down. At the break I was ready to throw in the towel. I said to Neil (who was filling in for DP): "Maybe today's the day he's going to beat me." Then I gave myself a metaphorical slap round the face. "No way! It's not going to be today," I said in the next breath.

After two hours and seven minutes of the bitterest and most exhausting squash we've ever played, I was 9-8 up in the fifth game. During a particularly gruelling rally I managed to force James to lunge full stretch into the front right corner to retrieve a forehand drop shot. His reply set me up perfectly in the front backhand with the whole court open to me. All I had to do was play a simple drop shot. Except, by then, I was knackered beyond belief, ready to drop. My thought processes had disintegrated and my racket grip was a sodden mess. So I did what anyone would do in the same situation: I thrashed the ball down the backhand wall as hard and as low as I possibly could. Fortunately James was so far out of position he didn't have the energy to recover. He flung himself to the floor in a desperate attempt to retrieve the ball, cramping in his leg so badly in the process that he was forced to retire from the match. I reckon my own legs had about 30 seconds before they themselves were going to succumb to cramping. I had never before cramped in my entire playing career. The match was that brutal. In the points leading up to James dropping out, I could feel my left hamstring twitching. He was hitting backhand drops that were off the planet, and forcing me to make lunges so deep I wasn't sure I could get back up from them. When he fell, at first I was worried he had done some serious damage. He was writhing around in agony. I didn't know if he'd pulled his hamstring or rolled over on his ankle. When he finally retired with cramp, I immediately thought "This isn't the way to close out a great match". But thank God he stayed down. I don't think I would have lasted another second myself.

I would much prefer that match to define our career rivalry rather than the 2009 British Open. I know it's a cliché but it really was an iconic battle. There was no sledging, no shenanigans between us, totally clean. We both played to the very highest level either of us could – and simultaneously. That's a very rare occurrence in this sport. We knocked seven bells out of each other and, at the end, neither of us was left standing.

The following day – after about five hours of treatment on my feet which felt like they had broken glass in them – I recovered to beat Gregory Gaultier 3-1 in the final. The squash wasn't as pretty as against James, though, after what we'd been through the night before, it was perhaps my finest example of using mind over matter to triumph. But it was that semi-final with James that will always stick in my memory. Of my entire career it is perhaps the match I look back on with the most fondness.

I always have to fight whenever I play James. Even though, as I write this, I'm on a long winning streak against him, every time I walk on court to face him, I see it as a clean slate – an equal chance for both of us to triumph. If you go on court expecting to win then you're already at a disadvantage because of your complacency. I use that mentality to make myself believe that one day I will break my losing streak against world No.1 Ramy Ashour. Every match is a new match, with new chances to outfox your opponent and new chances to win.

***

Reading back through this, I can see that it may look like James and I are permanently at each other's throats. That's not correct. Sometimes, when the weapons are safely stowed in the racket bags, we can actually be quite amicable, even gentlemanly, towards each other. It shouldn't be forgotten that the rivalry between us almost defines our careers. The sum of us both is greater than the individual parts. As much as we have our differences, as much as we feud, we have to admit we have constantly pushed each other to perform better. That's good for us and that's good for British squash.

CHAPTER 13

Dirty Sanchez

In which our champion fires a squash ball at a naked player's arse, endures the bear-pit atmosphere of French fans and finally gives James Willstrop a man hug.

In an individual sport like squash, where you spend most of the year competing just for yourself, it's refreshing to join forces with other players for an international team event. The strongest England team I've ever been part of was at the 2004 European Team Championships in the French city of Rennes. At No.1 we had Peter Nicol, Lee Beachill at No.2, me at No.3 and James Willstrop at No.4. We were unstoppable. There were around 3,000 Frenchmen spectating – at the time, it was the loudest and most partisan crowd I've ever competed in front of. Yet we still managed to hammer the French in the final, all of us victorious in half an hour or less. It must have been humiliating for them to get beaten so soundly on home soil.

What struck me most about that tournament was the incredible camaraderie that all our team members had. Bizarrely, one of the things that most bonded us all together was watching a DVD series called Dirty Sanchez. It's about this group of crazy Welshmen (and one Englishman) who carry out all sorts of sado-masochistic (and usually very gross) stunts. You know the sort of thing – hammering nails into their own body parts, setting their hair on fire and swallowing objects that humans are definitely not designed to swallow. It's not big, it's not clever, but it's totally hilarious. Anyway, perhaps because Dirty Sanchez involves a team of young men choosing to put themselves through serious pain, we, as squash players, related to it. We watched loads of episodes. In the end we decided that if we won the European Team Championships we would have to do a Dirty Sanchez-style forfeit each. Not quite in the same league as the professionals on the DVD – we didn't intend to set anyone's hair on fire – but something suitably painful and humiliating, all the same. When we weren't training or competing that week, we spent much of our time devising various torturous forfeits for each other. Ironic though it sounds, the whole process bonded the team more closely together.

After that final against the hosts, we were so delighted to win – and by such a margin – that the pain of a forfeit was something we were quite happy to bear. As No.1 in our team, Peter Nicol was first up. His forfeit was to be slapped hard across the face by Adrian Grant. Poor Adrian was only 23 at the time and Peter, seven years older, was very much still a sporting idol of his. He couldn't bring himself to slap his hero across the face. Peter sat in front of him, his face clenched, ready for the pain, yelling at Adrian, "Do it! Do it!" Eventually Peter had to grab Adrian by the testicles to make him react, at which he did "do it", striking Peter so hard that there was an imprint of Adrian's hand on his face for the next few hours.

My forfeit was to be whipped by Lee Beachill on my bare arse with a wet towel. Beach, as we call him, comes across as a bit of a dour Yorkshireman, but he was certainly the life and soul of the team back in those days. Peter was the eldest and led by example, but Beach was certainly the ring-leader. Needless to say, he had been honing his towel-whipping technique all week. His backhand was so strong that, while practising, he had actually managed to chip one of the tiles off the wall in the hotel bathroom. When it came to my whipping time, the force of the blow was so great it knocked me off my feet and left a huge welt on my backside for weeks afterwards.

That week of Dirty Sanchez-inspired forfeits set something of a precedent for the England team. Now, any time a player makes his debut for the national side, he has to undergo a sort of firing squad. But instead of rifles and bullets, he has to submit to a squash ball struck hard and fast at his naked backside. It's a fairly straightforward execution and never fails to draw a large crowd of spectators. The England debutant stands up against the front wall of a court with his shorts pulled down. All the other team members put their names in a hat and once the executioner's name has been chosen at random, he stands on the T and delivers the killer blow. My name was drawn to smack a ball at the naked behind of Tom Richards on his initiation in 2012. (Much to his dismay – he'd been hoping for a far less vicious executioner.) So I warmed up my swing, took aim and smacked the ball with all my might. Would you believe it? I missed. The ball struck the front wall just between Tom's legs, missing his crotch by millimetres. I was the first person in the history of the England team initiation ceremony ever to miss. Can you imagine how humiliating that was? I'd failed to hit his naked arse from a few yards away. I was world champion at the time and squash players have big arses. I'll never live it down.

***

When athletes from an individual sport unite as a team, it always arouses much debate. Is it crucial that you should bond off the court like a football team? Or is it better to concentrate on being a group of individuals? After all, even in team squash, it's your individual match that contributes to the overall team result. You can have the best team spirit in the world but if you don't deliver on court independently from your teammates, it all counts for nothing.

During my career wearing an England shirt, from my debut in 2003 up until the present day, our team has had many ups and downs. We've won the European Team Championships an incredible 10 times in a row. It's in the World Team Championships, however (staged every two years), that we are truly tested and ultimately judged. In 2003, in Vienna, on my debut, we had the misfortune of losing to France in the semi-finals, with Lee Beachill coming to grief in the deciding rubber to a young and very vociferous Gregory Gaultier. In 2005, in Islamabad, and in 2007, in Chennai, we won the world title. It was during this period (with Dirty Sanchez often in the DVD player) that our team spirit was at its strongest, blending the experience of the likes of Peter Nicol and Lee Beachill with the relative youth of James Willstrop, Peter Barker and me. Maybe we took this spirit for granted because in the following World Team Championships it all went horribly wrong.

The 2009 event was held in Odense in Denmark, hot on the heels of the British Open final. As you now know, James Willstrop and I were hardly best of buddies back then. In the aftermath of that infamous match James had said one or two things to the squash media that I really didn't agree with. Yes, I admit I'd gone overboard with my on-court comments about his dad, but it certainly wasn't the worst thing ever uttered on a squash court. To me, James's post-match reaction smacked of sour grapes. Had he won the match, instead of me, I'm sure my remark would have been forgotten about almost instantly.

So it was up to DP (both national coach and my individual coach at the time) to keep the peace. A tricky job, I'm sure. As the World Team Championships were approaching, he suggested James and I spoke on the phone to resolve our differences. That turned out to be a real comedy of errors. Firstly, neither of us is particularly good at answering the phone. At least a dozen times we tried to get hold of each other, playing this long drawn out game of answerphone squash, leaving ever more awkward messages for each other. When we finally spoke, our actual conversation was even more awkward. After half an hour we agreed to disagree. My opinion was that what goes on court should stay on court. I thought that in time we might perhaps get on again, whereas James felt our relationship had broken down for good. I now realise we of course both needed to grow up and, for the sake of the team, find some sort of happy medium. But with emotions running raw at the time, we found this very difficult.

Once the team squash had started, the animosity between James and me was obvious, and the atmosphere in our team camp uncomfortable. Matters went from bad to worse when, lunging for a ball in our second-day pool match against Germany, I twisted my left ankle and ruptured the ligaments. I spent the rest of that night in hospital, returning the following day on crutches. In a great deal of pain, I had to drop out of the event. To top things off, my replacement, Alister Walker, had fallen out with another team member, Adrian Grant, a few days earlier while playing in Cairo. So they weren't talking to each other either. Picture the situation: one guy on crutches, four guys blanking one another and a coach tearing his hair out. It was an utter shambles. We came fourth overall, lucky to finish even that high.

In 2011 the World Team Championships were staged in the German city of Paderborn. I honestly believe that was the best-organised squash tournament I have ever attended. Talk about German efficiency. This was around the time when the squash bid for the 2020 Olympics was first starting to take shape, so we were lucky to be competing on a brand-new, electric blue all-glass court with an accompanying light show. All around town the municipal buses had posters of giant squash players plastered across them.

Our opening match was against the hosts, Germany, with home support you can only describe as ear-splitting. Long gone were the days of "Quiet during play, please". The atmosphere during these matches – especially when German players took to the court – was more like for football than squash. And, in my opinion, the tournament was all the better for it. Under the guidance of our new England national coach – an affable Aussie and former world No.2 called Chris Robertson – we finished as runners-up. But it wouldn't be until two years later that we fully revived the team spirit that had seen us so strong in years past.

The 2013 World Team Championships were in Mulhouse, in eastern France. Local support came out in force, notably in the semi-final when we took on the hosts. Remember that 3,000-strong French crowd we had to contest with at Rennes in 2004? That was a walk in the park compared to Mulhouse. Whenever a French player won a point, the cheering was so loud it felt like you were physically lifted off your seat.

I was No.1 for our team, first match on against home favourite Gregory Gaultier. During the knock-up we were subjected to a particularly noisy rendition of the French national anthem, La Marseillaise. There were around 2,000 spectators but it sounded more like 10,000. Absolutely deafening. During the match, any time I asked for a let decision, I was met with a chorus of boos. It really was the most hostile crowd I have ever competed in front of. And bear in mind that our French neighbours really aren't that keen on the English, even at the best of times. Combine this natural animosity with the fact that temperatures that day reached 30 degrees Centigrade and you'll understand why it felt like a cauldron inside that venue.

Greg and I shared the first four games in our match. After two hours of play both of us started to suffer from cramp. At one point I felt like I'd been shot by a sniper in the back of my calf. (Surely even the French wouldn't resort to that.) With Greg 9-7 up in the fifth game, suddenly he hit the floor with a scream and started writhing around in agony. The referee informed him in no uncertain terms that, since he had used his injury time-out earlier in the match, he would have to forfeit the match. I was awarded victory. You should have heard the booing. You also should have witnessed how quickly Greg jumped back to his feet when the referee announced the match forfeit. Like a football striker who'd dived in the penalty box and was now prepared to take the penalty. Like Lazarus back from the dead.

Mind you, there was no way I was going to accept victory on a forfeit. In any sport, that just isn't the correct way to win. Given how absolutely knackered I was, I was tempted for perhaps a split second but I know I wouldn't have been able to live with myself. Also, I don't think I'd have escaped the building alive.

With Greg's cramp now worse than mine, I won the fifth game 12-10 after 138 minutes of play. It is, to date, the longest match of my entire career.

Greg was incredibly gracious in defeat, applauding me as I made a bit of a tit of myself, jumping around the court and celebrating like Bugs Bunny. I have a photo of me leaping in the air with the England team reacting just as excitedly behind me. The French team are seated next to them, all with their heads in their hands. That image will stay with me forever. And, unfortunately for my wife Esme, it will probably end up hung on our living-room wall.

In the next match James Willstrop beat Thierry Lincou to take us to the final. Play didn't finish until two o'clock in the morning. A very late dinner ended with over 500 remaining French supporters giving us a standing ovation. When you consider that they'd been booing us hours earlier, it was a remarkable turnaround and an amazing gesture of sportsmanship. The scene of devastation in our physio Jade's room after that semi-final was something to behold. James was writhing on the bed in pain, having his thighs massaged, while I lay on the floor, drifting in and out of consciousness, with acupuncture needles sticking out of my calves. In the background an ice bath was being prepared. I can safely say that was the first time – and hopefully the last – I've ever submerged myself in an ice bath at 3.30 in the morning.

The following day we won our final against Egypt 2-1. I lost my individual match against Ramy, but Daryl Selby played out of his skin and James sealed the title. What an incredible feeling to lift that world trophy again, this time as team captain. I had been No.4 in the team in 2005, No.1 in 2007 and finally captain in 2013. Three World Team titles. And it felt so much better that we'd been forced to win it the hard way. It was a real team effort from the players, the coaches and the support staff. Perhaps the most remarkable thing of the entire week was that James and I found ourselves hugging each other after our win – and again as we said goodbye at the airport. We had performed our individual tasks brilliantly but, most rewardingly, we had reunited as a team. We had found that England spirit again.

***

I'm proud to say that I've always loved playing for my country. I now have close to 100 caps under my belt. The highest honour of all was being England captain. Winning titles as part of a team gives you a totally different feeling to winning individual titles. We squash players can be very selfish individuals and it's only once or twice in the whole year that we get the opportunity to combine as a team. Without wishing to sound cheesy, there really is something special about sharing victory with other players who have been through the same emotions and experiences as you. A truly rewarding experience.

CHAPTER 14

The other half

In which we see Nick eschewing a life of sheep-farming, wooing his future wife in between emergency trips to the toilet and hiding the engagement ring beneath a fairy's dress.

I spent most of my first date with Esme sprinting to and from the toilet. It wasn't the most auspicious start to our relationship.

It was my own fault, though, since I'd under-cooked a piece of chicken a few days before. Pale, sweaty and sick, eruptions from both ends. Imagine what Esme must have thought as we sat across the table from each other in a smart restaurant. The conversation kept getting interrupted each time I staggered to the gents.

Esme and I had first met a few years before that. She was a 22-year-old intern at the English Institute of Sport in Manchester. I was 27 and on the cusp of making it big time in squash. She was a bit of an EIS dogsbody at the time. Several squash players had gone to Manchester to do a fitness session with heart-rate monitors and she was noting down the results. I remember thinking she was great looking. But she had a boyfriend and I had a girlfriend so I assumed nothing would come of it.

My girlfriend back then was Hannah Lewis, a tennis coach at Hallamshire. Hannah and I had dated briefly in our teenage years and had got back together a few years later. We had a lot in common through our mutual involvement in racket sports. I got on really well with her parents and it was the first relationship in which I felt part of someone else's family. This was a big thing, I guess, for an only child. I think the emotion of our relationship was even greater because her mother was going through cancer at the time and we both shared the trauma of that experience.

The problem was Hannah wasn't happy being a tennis coach. In fact, she hated her job. She had been coaching since the age of 16 and was now fed up with the early mornings and repetitive lessons. She needed a change. Her dream, of all things, was to be a farmer instead. At first she started growing vegetables, which was great for Sunday lunches, with all the trimmings straight from the garden. But then she took things a step further, packing in the coaching altogether and keeping sheep instead. Her aim was to be a proper shepherdess.

In the early days she would keep the sheep in her back garden, so their bleating would often keep us awake during the night. During lambing season she had to get up every few hours during the night to check on them. I think it was around this time that I stopped spending the night at her place. Nocturnal bleating is hardly the best preparation for a squash tournament.

Hannah had hopes that, once I'd retired from professional squash, I'd join her working on a farm. I suppose I could just about live off the land but I certainly couldn't muck in with all the animals. I don't like early mornings, let alone getting my fingernails dirty. Shortly after that Hannah and I went our separate ways.

For the next couple of years I pretty much stayed single. I had fun with a few girls but I never got tied down in a relationship. It's really tough for a professional sportsman to have a serious girlfriend, especially if your sport involves an international tour as squash does. Our season lasts for eight or nine months a year, during which I'm out of the country for at least two weeks in every month. It can be difficult for a romantic relationship to survive that.

To be successful in a professional racket sport you need to be exceedingly self-absorbed. Imagine I'm over in the United States, preparing for a major tournament. I can't take a day off to go shopping with my girlfriend in New York, or to visit the Grand Canyon. To have any chance of faring well, I need to focus 100 per cent on my imminent matches. I have to train, rest, sleep, eat, drink and prepare my equipment with total precision. The only person I'm thinking about (other than myself) is my next opponent. What possible fun would I be as a companion for my girlfriend? I suppose that's why so many professional athletes end up dating people from their own sport. That way they understand what their other half is going through and they can synchronise their work time and play time.

With that in mind, when Esme and I finally did get it together, I don't suppose I imagined it would last that long. It was just before the Delhi Commonwealth Games in 2010. I was having dinner in Manchester with my manager, Paul, when a text message came through from my physio, Jade. "I know a certain blonde who really likes you," she texted rather intriguingly. After that Esme and I did a bit of text flirting and eventually organised a dinner date – the one where I spent less time talking to her and more to the great white telephone because of food poisoning.

A few weeks later, just as our relationship was gaining momentum, I had to fly to India for the Games. I was away for three and a half weeks. This was Esme's first taste of what it was like to date a travelling athlete. But I was determined to keep the affair going, so we talked on the mobile phone and via Skype every day I was away. We weren't allowed to tell anyone else we were dating. The EIS really disapproves of their employees getting involved with any of the athletes they work with – there was a clause in their contracts forbidding it. In fact Esme had to seek special permission from her bosses before we could make our relationship public knowledge. Since she mainly worked with cyclists, not squash players, they made an exception.

During the build-up to Delhi, my stomach – and match preparations – were in a mess. Sick as a dog, I did what many only children do in such situations: I moved back to my parents' house so that my mum could look after me. Despite my mum's protests, I was so desperate to go on that date with Esme that I ended up making myself more ill in the process. That sort of thing tends to happen when you inflict steak and red wine upon a poorly stomach.

I'd already had to withdraw from the British Grand Prix in Manchester and now I was so ill I couldn't train for over two weeks. All confidence in my fitness had evaporated. It all came to a head the Monday before we were due to fly when my trainer, Mark Campbell, and the main strength and conditioning coach for England Squash, a chap called Matt Cook, decided to give me a fitness test. This was a risky move by them. If my results were poor, I would arrive in Delhi with my confidence at its lowest ebb. Mark and Matt put me through gruelling sets of repetitive on-court ghosting moves and my results came out better than ever before. The risk had paid off. (Mark has since confided in me that they were prepared to lie to me about my results if necessary. Anything for me to get over the psychological hurdle.)

The next day I was very sore but I finally felt ready to represent my country in the Commonwealth Games.

I was so psychologically desperate to win the singles, having come fourth and just missed out on a medal at the previous Commonwealth Games in Melbourne in 2006. On that occasion I lost to Peter Nicol in the semi-finals and it had devastated me. There was no way I was going to settle for anything less than gold in Delhi. I know it's a cliché but, much like Peter four years earlier, I truly believed it was my destiny. The draw was incredibly favourable for me, too. Four Englishmen – James Willstrop, Peter Barker, Daryl Selby and I – occupied the top four seed positions, but there was danger lurking in the form of Aussie David Palmer. So when I saw that David had been drawn in James's quarter of the draw I was more than happy.

Since squash doesn't feature in the Olympics, the Commonwealth Games is seen as a sort of mini-Olympic Games for our sport. If you ever have any doubt as to how important this event is you need only watch the Peter Nicol vs David Palmer final in Melbourne. I can honestly say that is the most inspiring squash match I have ever had the privilege to witness. Home favourite Palmer played out of his skin, yet Englishman Nicol still managed to soak up everything he threw at him and eventually broke him three games to one in front of 3,000 hostile Aussies. I think that match gave me the psychological inspiration I needed to win gold four years later in Delhi.

I stuttered through the early stages of the draw, perhaps understandably given the food poisoning I'd endured in the previous weeks, so my confidence wasn't high as I entered the latter stages. I've always maintained that to be successful in any tournament you shouldn't peak in the first round but (providing you get through) try to gain momentum and improve your performances round by round. This is easier said than done. Delhi certainly put my theory to the test. After a first-round bye, I dropped a couple of games in the second and third rounds to lower-ranked players. My parents had travelled to Delhi, along with my Auntie Sue, and as they sat in the crowd I could see the worried expressions on their faces. My aunt later told me how the most worrying thing of all was the nasty grey complexion I was sporting. But as we got into the business end of the tournament, I seemed to get stronger and stronger by the day. From the quarter-finals to winning the gold medal, I played some of the best squash of my career, not dropping a single game.

In major tournaments, as you feel the finishing line approaching, something really strange happens in your mind. All throughout your training, your coach tells you how crucial it is to focus only on the next point. Yet, imagine you're three points away from victory in the Commonwealth Games. The temptation to think about that gold medal is too great. Suddenly your entire career flashes through your mind – the juniors, all the coaching, all the gruelling workouts, all the tournaments, your parents, your friends, the high points, the low points, everything is relived in a split second. It's what I imagine people experience in the nanoseconds before the impact of a car crash. But, of course, to close out the match you need to remain entirely focused. You have to block all these life memories out of your mind. You can't let yourself think that you're about to win, that it's Commonwealth or Olympic gold hanging in the balance. You have to think about the "processes not the outcome", as my sports psychologist often says. You have to trick your mind that it's just another ordinary point within the match. And that is why athletes look so gobsmackingly surprised when they finally do win. If you ever see a video clip of me winning gold in Delhi you'll see just how astounded I was.

I also won gold in the doubles event. Now, let's be honest about doubles squash. It's a pretty dull spectacle. Yes, they widen the court and shorten matches to best-of-three but it still tends to be overly attritional, often tedious. Play a practice match and you get nice, freely flowing points. But when there are medals at stake it turns into a hack-fest with loads of lets. No one, neither players nor ref, seems to know what constitutes a stroke and what constitutes a let.

We singles players are an intense, selfish lot and the idea of competing as a doubles team is pretty alien. At the 2006 Commonwealth Games I teamed up with James Willstrop. As we quickly learned, you can both be among the strongest singles players in the world but if you don't communicate effectively then you don't stand a chance. We bombed out in the quarter-finals to a pair of Kiwis called Campbell Grayson and Martin Knight who were, at the time, both ranked outside the world top 100 in singles. They communicated brilliantly, however, and stuffed us.

So when it came to the 2010 Commonwealth doubles I was determined to get the right partner. I ended up teamed with my good friend Adrian Grant. We were mates both on the court and off it. I'm a rightie, he's a leftie, so we could both concentrate on our forehand sides. In the run-up to the Games we got some invaluable advice from badminton doubles star Gail Emms. Winner of Olympic silver and five Commonwealth medals, she certainly knew what she was talking about. She basically told us: "Leave your egos off the court. Just because you're good at singles doesn't mean you're any good at doubles." She explained that in badminton she would be lucky to win just a few points playing the world No.1 singles player and, likewise, the world No.1 singles player would struggle to get points off her in doubles.

Gail taught Adrian and me how to communicate properly. She sat us back to back and gave one of us a picture of a random pattern and the other a pencil. One of us would then describe the pattern verbally while the other would draw what he imagined was being described. We were pretty useless at this task, ending up with an image completely different to the original. But we grasped the message: communication was key.

Adrian and I decided we would communicate in between every single point of our doubles matches. We would whisper strategies or encouragement or congratulations. Anything, as long as we exchanged words, or even a positive nod, between each point. It made such a psychological difference to each match. Now I know why, in tennis and badminton, doubles partners tap hands in between points. It used to annoy me, watching this endless hand tapping, but finally I understood the benefits. Even if there's nothing to say, it acts as a reminder that you're a team, that someone is watching out for you, that someone is always there to back you up.

And it worked. Adrian and I took gold. Adrian was in sensational form all week. I was slightly tired from the individual event and he carried me on his shoulders all the way through. Other teams had wrongly assumed that due to our respective singles rankings (I was ranked No.2 in the world at the time whereas Adrian was No.14) Adrian would be the weakest link. How wrong could they be? He was on fire and won our Man of the Match award every single day.

Unfortunately for the spectators (those that were left by that stage) doubles makes for incredibly dull squash. Each match simply became a war of attrition. We'd totally worked out the tactics for winning at doubles squash. Although we tried our best to attack as much as possible, ultimately it's all about which partnership keeps the rallies going longest and which communicates best.

Once we'd secured gold, a guy from the World Squash Federation came up to us and said: "Thank God that's finished!" After all the effort we'd expended, I thought Adrian was going to throttle him. We'd just bust our guts in a sport he'd essentially helped to design. If it was boring then it was his fault, not ours. We had tried our best to make it exciting – an impossible task.

Those Delhi Games received a lot of negative media coverage back home. The surface of the athletics track, for example, had been laid out only hours before the Games started, while one of the spectator bridges collapsed. Some of the swimmers picked up bugs from the water in the swimming pool. I particularly remember Francesca Halsall, the English freestyle and butterfly swimmer, looking like she might keel over after one of her swims. The athletes' accommodation was hardly five-star but I suppose that depends on what you were expecting. On the squash tour we travel a lot to the Asian subcontinent, so we perhaps knew what to expect more than some of the other athletes did.

The food, however, was superb: a vast food tent open 24 hours a day, full of all of the world's cuisines and a very tempting dessert station. Pete Barker decided to sample a different doughnut every day during the early part of the tournament. But we were soon all eating healthily. There was of course a great Indian food section which, wary of food poisoning, we avoided until the final night of the Games when we celebrated with a spicy curry soaked with numerous beers.

I heard a few stories about infestations of rats and cockroaches in some of the athletes' rooms. Fortunately there was nothing like that in our apartment. The South African squash team told us they once returned to their room to find the cleaner merrily brushing his teeth with one of their toothbrushes.

The biggest nightmare in Delhi was the fiasco over ticket sales. Some venues were advertised as sold out yet, when play started, there were hundreds of empty seats. Daryl Selby had to rush out of the venue during Pete Barker's bronze medal match to help Pete's mum get into the venue. Even though the seats were half-empty, officials wouldn't let her in and she was panicking that she might miss her son's proudest moment. Later on there were reports of thousands of unused corporate tickets found in landfills all over the city.

I arrived jubilant back in the UK from Delhi but was quickly brought back down to earth. We travelled home on the same flight as the diver Tom Daley. While Tom had paparazzi following him everywhere across Heathrow Airport, no one was vaguely interested in me. Along with Tom and Rebecca Adlington, I was one of only three English athletes to win double gold in Delhi but, as usual, the squash player got no coverage whatsoever. I was so frustrated at how anonymous I was on my return. For once in my life I wanted to be recognised. On my way to the underground station, still in team uniform, two passers-by asked me how I'd got on in Delhi. I lacked the heart to tell them about the two gold medals safely stashed away in my Team England rucksack.

***

Along with my two medals, my biggest souvenir from Delhi was a ferocious phone bill from all the calls I'd been making to Esme. When I'd first travelled out there I'd worried that perhaps a new girlfriend would be a distraction from my task of winning medals. But as I flew back I realised it must have helped me. You know that warm glow you get when you first start getting serious with a girlfriend? Plus I had someone to talk to every day while I was out in Delhi.

The day after I arrived back in the UK, Esme and Jade organised a gold-themed party specially for me. They had secretly invited loads of our friends, all of whom were sporting gold medals, wigs and sunglasses. You can imagine how great it was to have everyone close to me celebrating those two medals. Given the distance and costs, only my parents and Auntie Sue had been able to fly out to Delhi to support me. That won't be the case if I end up competing at the Commonwealth Games in Glasgow in 2014. There will be plenty of home support for that, I'm certain.

After Delhi, Esme and I started dating properly and full-time. One of us would regularly make the commute between Sheffield and Manchester, over Snake Pass. After a year or so, any time I was back in the UK, Esme would stay at my place in Sheffield. Yet we didn't quite want to make that full commitment of her moving in, so all she had in the way of personal space was a drawer for her clothes and a few hangers in the wardrobe. It was quite a small house that I lived in anyway.

Towards the end of 2011 we decided to find a new place together. With her working every day in Manchester and me training in Sheffield, we faced a bit of a dilemma. Which city should we set up house together in? What about somewhere in between? There's not much between Manchester and Sheffield except for hills and moorland and lots of sheep. And you already know what I think of sheep.

I really needed to be near my training base at Hallamshire. Esme needed to get to the EIS in Manchester every day. In the end we opted for our house on the south-west edge of Sheffield, near a railway station that links quickly to Manchester. So I fared better out of the compromise but it's still an easy commute for Esme.

In June 2013 we tied the knot. Our wedding was in a lovely little village called Grindleford, in the Peak District, not far from Sheffield. Despite never having the slightest doubts about marrying Esme, I was more nervous waiting for her to walk down the aisle than I'd ever been for any squash match. Of course I couldn't resist sneaking a look behind me and was totally blown away when I saw her in her wedding dress. She looked so beautiful that I was lost for words. (That's a first for me.) The experience of my wedding day makes any squash match pale into insignificance. It was very humbling for me to sit at the top table at the reception and look out at all the faces I know and love. Peter Fantich, an ex-training partner, had travelled all the way from Australia; Beau River, another DP protégé, all the way from Chicago. It struck me that all of these people would never be in the same room together ever again. Peter

Barker later texted me to say it was the happiest he had ever seen me. He was, of course, right. It was the best day of our lives. The only problem was it flashed by far too quickly.

Beforehand, there was of course a stag party, too. That was in London, in March 2013, after the Canary Wharf Classic. We had originally wanted to go away somewhere flamboyant like for Peter Barker's stag do in Las Vegas in 2011, but unfortunately the squash schedule wouldn't allow it. So the plan instead was to go out on the Saturday night after the Canary Wharf Classic had finished. A few of my mates arrived a day early so they could (they hoped) watch me in the tournament final on the Friday night. Perhaps the fear of the practical jokes they might subject me to on my stag do was weighing on my mind because I never made it past the semi-finals. The bonus was that my stag party ended up spread over two nights instead of one. And I was spared any severe practical jokes.

***

Esme is always busy with her job so she has little time to waste watching me sweat it out on court. She does, however, support me any time I'm competing in the UK and maybe for the odd tournament abroad if she can get time off work. It would be ridiculous to expect her to follow me any more than that.

I've never understood how the WAGs of professional sportsmen (golfers, say, or tennis players or footballers) can sit loyally through every single match their other half competes in. Surely, as much as they love their husband and the sport he plays, they must get bored after a few years of the same old rigmarole? Imagine having to freeze your proverbials off watching Mansfield Town every week. Or spending your weekends following every shot that Jim Furyk plays. I think I'd have more fun watching paint dry. That would be like a hedge fund manager expecting his wife to come to his office every day and watch him work.

In Esme's case, even if she did want to watch live every single ball I struck in anger, her job means she couldn't travel everywhere that I do. As I said, I'm out of the country every two weeks out of four for nine months of the year.

Once, after paying a particularly eye-watering tax bill, I made a note of how many days I spent outside the UK. To be a tax exile you have to live in the country for fewer than 183 days a year. One year, when I was travelling more than usual, I clocked up a total of 132 days abroad, so I wasn't even close. To be honest, I don't think I earn enough to make it worthwhile staying abroad for those extra 50-odd days anyway. I'd rather be at home and pay more tax. What a model citizen I am, hey?

People often ask if those long periods of separation put pressure on our relationship. Before the invention of Skype and smartphones, that might have been the case. But now that we can communicate so easily every day, we never really feel that far apart. Don't get me wrong, I would rather be at home with Esme, and I hope she'd rather have me around, but she knows I have an important job to do. She knows the commitment I have to make to remain among the world's best squash players. She has an important job to do, too.

When you compete in a knockout tournament sport like squash, there's a strange dynamic at play. If Esme hopes for me to come home soon, essentially she's hoping for me to lose early in a tournament. So, ironically, she has to hope I'll be away for longer. The longer I'm away, by definition, the more successful I am.

Some professional squash players have relationships with female players on the women's WISPA tour. That way, when PSA and WISPA tournaments coincide (actually quite rare), they can spend time together. I could never share my life with another squash professional. It wouldn't be healthy. It would be far too intense. What makes Esme so perfect for me is that she understands sport – she used to row in national competitions when she was younger and now works in cycling at Olympic level. The women's team pursuit squad she works with, including Laura Trott, Dani King and Joanna Rowsell, won gold at the London Olympics. Fortunately Esme's not immersed in squash like I am. It means we have a healthy balance to our marriage. Imagine if we were both squash pros and we went home together every night and chatted for hours about our sport. We'd go crazy after a few weeks. Besides, I have enough squash to worry about with my own career. If I was dating another squash pro I'd have two squash careers to worry about.

Esme is brilliant for me. The first thing you notice about her is her hair – long, blonde and curly. It's probably what initially attracted me to her. Hopefully our kids will be curly blondes too. I've seen photos of Esme when she was younger and her hair was dead straight. Apparently she contracted glandular fever and woke up one morning to discover it had turned curly overnight.

She's the most caring and thoughtful person you're ever likely to meet. I always joke about how many greetings cards she buys for other people. Birthdays, anniversaries, pregnancies, Christmas, a new house, a new dog, a new haircut… it's endless. Someone will go to the toilet and she'll want to buy them a card in way of congratulations.

She was brought up in Cheshire, the third of four daughters. Occasionally she can be quite insecure which stems, I think, from losing her mum when she was young. This has brought her much closer to *my* mum, however. She loves the fact that my mum is so doting, loving and thoughtful to both of us. I remember the first time Esme and Sue spent the day together. Esme came home very happy and emotional afterwards. When you consider that her own mum passed away when she was just 17, that's understandable.

Esme and I got engaged in December 2012. Choosing the ring was quite a performance, I can tell you. I placed all my trust in a jeweller called Keith White I know down in the West Country, who managed to find the perfect rock and the perfect setting. Keeping it secret from Esme all the while, I had the ring couriered to me in Sheffield and then hid it on top of the Christmas tree in our living room, right next to the fairy. Somehow I engineered things so that Esme discovered it by chance on the tree. I'm proud to say that when she turned round I was genuflecting with appropriate chivalry on the floor. She was putty in my hands and agreed instantly.

Now that we're hitched, the next major life issue is kids. She is one of four siblings while I'm an only child. So a good compromise would be two or three kids. Any more than that is greedy.

CHAPTER 15

Taking on the pie-eaters

In which Nick receives his first pay cheque, wakes up
with another player's socks in his face and loses out to
the world pie-eating champion.

"Alberto not tough! He need more matches!"

Those words, back in 1998, were my lucky break in professional
squash. The man who said them was the father of a junior Spanish
player called Alberto Manso and the director of the first ever
professional tournament I played in: the 1998 Ciutat de Barcelona.
Rather than giving his son the wildcard into his own tournament,
he gave it to me instead. It was just the leg-up I needed.

Ángel Manso. I'll never forget that guy. Without him I might
have been floundering around the lower echelons of the PSA tour
for years. Instead, thanks to his wildcard, I got to the final of the
first professional tournament I competed in and catapulted myself
straight up the world rankings into the world top 250. It was the
perfect start to my career. Many fledgling pros spend their first year
on the tour languishing at 400 in the world.

So why did Ángel pick me out for his wildcard and make his own
son struggle through qualifying instead? He was probably returning
a favour since we used to have Alberto to stay in the family home
every year in Sheffield during the British Junior Open. Alberto was
a couple of years younger than me and his father genuinely thought
he needed more match practice.

In the end, both of us fared well in Barcelona. Alberto stormed
through qualifying and reached the first round, while my wildcard
status gave me a massive boost of confidence and enabled me to take
out the No.2 seed, Englishman Peter Genever, in the first round.

Things got even better from then on until I reached the tournament final where I lost to Finnish stalwart Olle Poutiainen. It was a brilliant debut. I received around US$500 in prize money – my first pay cheque as a professional player. It felt like I'd won the Lottery. It was unbelievably exciting. Finally I had proved that I could make a living from my sport. More importantly, my performance gave me a world ranking in the top 250 which meant I could now enter the qualifying rounds of major PSA events. Just one week as a professional and already I was running with the big boys.

Outside of the world top 50, earning a living through squash is a tough business. To give you an example, in the UK, the lowest rung of professional squash are the British Squash Professional Association tournaments, or BSPA. These are staged at various squash clubs around the country – we had one at Hallamshire in my early years as a pro. Win the tournament and you're looking at a handful of PSA ranking points and maybe a cheque for £500. Lose in the first round and you get a measly £10 or so. Not surprising, really, when you consider how few people watch matches at this level. In the early rounds, the only spectators are often the players' parents and the odd club member on his way to the toilets. When you factor in travel and accommodation costs, you quickly realise it's impossible to make a living competing in these events. Without sponsorship or federation funding, you'd be running at a massive loss.

I was incredibly fortunate as the year I turned pro coincided with the start of Lottery funding for sport. During my first year I received £6,000 in funding and had all my training, coaching, gym, physio, nutrition and massage costs covered. Without that I would have been racking up debts just to stay active on tour. It's unlikely even my lucky wildcard at the Ciutat de Barcelona, and the ensuing jump up the world rankings, would have improved my financial status very much.

This Lottery funding was indispensable. When I reached 18 years old my parents wanted me to go to university. Playing squash as a living was simply too risky, they said. But they could see how desperate I was to make it as a professional player. So all three of us negotiated an agreement. I would give squash my maximum effort for a couple of years and if I hadn't succeeded by then I would pack it in and do a degree course instead. We never really discussed the finer details of what defined my success. But when I reached the world top 50 in 2000, at the age of 20, going to university was never mentioned again. (I often wonder what I might have studied. Perhaps I could have combined my parents' teaching skills – English and sport – to do a course in sports journalism.)

Those first two years on the PSA tour were no walk in the park. Even with the £6,000 funding, and living with my parents to save on rent, I was still barely breaking even. There were a couple of sponsors on the scene. Prospec, the manufacturers of glass-backed squash courts, gave me a bit of support. Then I signed a racket deal with Dunlop which gave me free rackets and a little cash. That was thanks to my manager, Paul, who was working with Dunlop at the time.

This was when I first started to feel valued as a sportsman. Dunlop had headhunted me. They actually wanted to pay me to compete with their rackets. Imagine what a privilege and confidence boost that is when you're first starting out on the tour.

Nevertheless, when it came to travel and accommodation, I needed some serious scrimping. Whenever I travelled abroad it was on cheap economy flights. Once at the tournament, I would hook up with some of the other British pros. Sometimes, if we were lucky, we might crash on friends' sofas to save on hotel bills. The more prestigious tournaments would offer free hotel accommodation which, at that stage in my career, was the height of luxury. For the smaller events I would often join forces with other British players to find cheap bed and breakfast accommodation. Sometimes there would be four of us in a double room. Adrian Grant, now also one of the top-ranked English players, was a regular roommate of mine. On more than one occasion I would wake up with his feet in my face because we'd gone top-to-toe in the single bed of a bed and breakfast. All good character-building stuff. I still have nightmares about his cheesy feet, though.

On other occasions the tournament organisers might put us up with a local family. In those early days this was more often than not the most luxurious accommodation we had. Some of the squash families on the east coast of the USA, for example, live in houses the size of castles. Some of them even have their own squash courts.

These families treated us like they would their own kids, saving us loads of money in food and laundry bills. (Believe me, squash players have both insatiable appetites and a tendency to sweat profusely on court.) We were really made to feel at home there.

I remember with horror one occasion when I unintentionally abused this hospitality. One winter Adrian and I were staying with a lovely family near our tournament in Greenwich, Connecticut. They had reminded us dozens of times that their downstairs bathroom toilet was out of order. I'd been feeling unwell that week; so unwell, in fact, that I totally forgot their warnings about said dodgy toilet. Sure enough, the evidence of my illness wouldn't flush away. I was left in a rather awkward position. My shame was too great for me to notify the lady of the house so, desperate, I hunted around for something – anything – to remove the offending material. Nearby I found an antique picnic hamper with some lovely china crockery in it. Yes, it embarrasses me to admit that I used a beautiful china plate as a scoop. Afterwards I had to hide it in my squash bag for several hours until we got to the squash club, where fortunately I was able to bury it outside in a pile of snow. That week I was so ill that the tournament doctor wouldn't allow me to fly home. Every night I sweated profusely in my bed. My poor hostess not only had her best china ruined but also had to change my sweaty bed sheets every night. I'm sure she was eventually glad to see the back of me.

Other accommodation wasn't always so homely. Once, in Kuwait, we were housed in a rather strange student institute which hadn't quite been finished, with bare concrete walls and cheap bunk beds. I seriously worried the whole building might collapse in the middle of the night. The dilemma was: do you take the top bunk and risk falling five feet to the concrete floor? Or do you plump for the bottom bunk and risk having the player and bed above you crush you in your sleep? I opted for the bottom bunk with a small player sleeping above me.

It wasn't until I was 24 years old that I finally had enough financial independence to move out of my parents' house. The problem was that I was plagued with a recurrent back injury. I'd work really hard to put together a string of good tournament performances and then, bang, my back would fall apart. Out of the blue I'd get these brutally painful back spasms when it felt like someone had plunged a knife into my lower back. Sometimes, for a whole week, I wouldn't be able to put my shoes or socks on. So any PSA points I'd won, and any rungs I'd climbed up the rankings ladder, were then negated by these forced injury lay-offs. It was so frustrating. I seriously began to doubt whether I could actually make a living from squash. Without that Lottery funding I would have totally run out of money.

It turned out I had disc problems. Things became desperate. Eventually I hooked up with this brilliant physio at the English Institute of Sport in Sheffield called Rob Johnson. He was an ex-professional footballer, a right defender, so he completely understood the one-sided nature of a sport like squash. He would treat me, my back would be fine, but then six weeks later I'd be wracked in pain again from the spasms.

Finally, after Rob taught me to control the core muscles in my abdomen area, the spasms disappeared. I've had the odd relapse – the 2009 British Open springs to mind – but these episodes thankfully seem to be in the past.

The higher you get in the world rankings, the more media attention you get, and the more potential sponsors knock on your door. Don't get me wrong, in squash we don't command anywhere near the same sponsorship value as footballers, golfers or tennis players. But, once in the world top 10, there's a fair amount of money to be made.

2011, the year I reached world No.1, was so far the highest-earning season of my career. I know it's crass when people boast about how much they earn and the last thing I want to do is show off about my income. However, it's important if you want to understand how the sport works. In 2011 I earned about £100,000 in prize money and around the same amount in sponsorship deals. Dunlop remained my main sponsor, giving me a retainer as long as I kept myself inside the world top 50. They also gave me bonuses for winning major tournaments and reaching the world No.1 spot. Thanks to that I was able to put down a deposit for the house I now live in.

Hi-Tec shoes are a good sponsor, too. There's also an American resort on the east coast of Georgia, near the border with Florida, called Sea Island which has signed me as its touring pro. I use its squash facilities as my North American training base and have the odd holiday there. I'm incredibly lucky that they pay me if I attract lots of players to the squash camps that I run there a couple times a year. It truly is paradise on earth. (No, it really is. They haven't paid me to say that.) I also have smaller sponsors in Trion:Z (which produces those magnetic therapy bracelets and necklaces) and Rehband (manufacturers of compression training clothing).

Compared to the world's major sports, squash is very much the poor cousin, though. At the time of writing this, I was ranked in the world top four. Do you think my income was anywhere close to the world's top four footballers, golfers, tennis players, American footballers, baseballers, boxers, basketballers, or Formula 1 drivers? You've got to be insane if you think I earn anywhere near the likes of Cristiano Ronaldo, Rory McIlroy, Andy Murray, Peyton Manning, Alex Rodriguez, Manny Pacquiao, Kobe Bryant or Fernando Alonso. I'd guess that plenty of players in the FA's Football League Two earn more than I do. Rory McIlroy's caddie probably trousers more than me.

Not that I'm bitter. Please don't think that. I'm perfectly happy with my income. It's more than enough. As Esme constantly reminds me, we squash players spend our working days chasing a little black ball round a sweaty box. It's not like we're curing cancer or struggling for world peace. In relation to other essential professions we're bloody lucky. At the very top of the game, squash players earn more than teachers, doctors and nurses – which is hardly fair if you think about it.

I do believe squash players deserve more prize money, however, especially when you consider the physical and mental effort we give.

I remember reading a news article back in 2011 when I was world No.1 that compared the income of athletes from a wide variety of sports. I was gutted because they had me ranked down below the world pie-eating champion. Or was it the world hotdog-eating champion? In any case, he was fat, greedy and he earned more than I did. But the author of the article had taken into account only the prize money from each sport, ignoring the sponsorship earnings. I can't imagine hotdog-eaters garner much sponsorship. Factor in my Dunlop and Hi-Tec deals and I should have been much higher up the income scale. Next time you're munching on a hotdog, bear that in mind.

I don't want you to think I obsess about my income, however. I've always enjoyed a very comfortable lifestyle. With both parents as teachers, we were by no means minted. Then again, we never wanted for any essentials. Like most of the world's squash players, I come from an ordinary middle-class family. Neither rich nor poor.

I won't deny that I've occasionally wished squash players were paid more – me included. Players ranked outside the world top 50 have to scrimp and save to make a living. They may hail from an African or South American country where sponsors are non-existent. You can hardly expect the likes of Dunlop, Wilson, Prince or Karakal to give cash and free rackets to a lower-ranked player from Zimbabwe or Paraguay who never makes the newspapers, in a country where only a handful of his compatriots are likely to buy a squash racket, let alone play regularly.

Worry too much about what you earn, however, and it can eat away at you. If I really wanted to pocket Tiger Woods-style pay cheques (over $78 million a year, last time I checked), I wouldn't have chosen squash as a career. I play squash because I love squash. I've never been the kind of person who is driven by money. I've never found myself thinking, "If I win this match then I'll get a cheque for 10 grand". That would be totally the wrong way to approach the sport – and a mindset that would prevent me from winning anyway. I can tell you that the day I start thinking like that will be the day I cease to be a top player. That's because, if I'm preoccupied with how much my next pay cheque is, it follows that I'm no longer backing myself to reach tournament finals. "Concentrate on the things you can control and everything else will take care of itself." That's one of my mottoes.

The main reason there's not more money in squash is simple: television. We're not on it enough. So our sponsors don't get as much of a return for their investment as football or golf or tennis sponsors do. It's not rocket science. Tiger Woods, Roger Federer and Cristiano Ronaldo appear on prime time TV channels for hours on end, their sponsors' logos glinting under the cameras. We squash players, on the other hand, only appear regularly on a paid-for internet TV channel – Squash TV. Relatively few viewers see us. Even fewer see our sponsors' logos. To secure more investment, squash needs to be on major TV channels more often. We now have one tournament a year – the World Series Finals in January – live on Sky Sports, and highlights packages two or three times a month. Squash makes it onto other channels around the world such as Total Sports Asia, Eurosport, STAR Sports and ESPN. But, compared to other sports, it's few and far between. The marketing men in the sport need to persuade TV executives that squash matches make for exciting drama. And that takes time.

I suppose I could have become a professional tennis player instead. As a kid, tennis was my first sport, long before squash. And I wasn't bad at it. Of course, because of all the money and extra investment, there are thousands more tennis pros in the world than there are squash pros. You could argue that I might never have made it to world No.1 had I chosen a fluffy yellow ball instead of a small, rubbery one. But I know just how driven I am. If I'd gone into tennis as a career, I don't know if I would have reached the very top of the rankings. I think I would have got somewhere close, though. I never would have allowed myself to settle for anything less. Even if my greatest talent had been tiddlywinks or Scrabble, I would have busted a gut, sweated blood, to be the very best in the world. When I watch my football club Sheffield Wednesday boot the ball around the Football League Championship I imagine that I could have been good enough to play in the midfield for them. Alright, that's a bit of a pipe dream. But with tiddlywinks and Scrabble, I'm deadly serious.

It's strange that my club, Hallamshire, has produced me, a double world squash champion, and Jonny Marray, a Wimbledon doubles champion. I started off playing tennis and switched to squash. Jonny started off playing squash and switched to tennis. Both of us excelled in our second choices.

I never discovered a real love for tennis, though. Not like I have in squash. I remember going to local tennis tournaments when I was eight, nine and 10 years old. When I wasn't playing I'd be sitting in my parents' car, watching the other matches through a wire fence. The other kids and parents were always a bit sceptical about newcomers. They didn't appear to want to make friends. It was quite a hostile atmosphere at times.

Squash, though, was a breath of fresh air. It was far more convivial, much more fun. All the players and parents were friendly.

When we weren't competing, we'd all gather on the spare courts – sometimes 10 kids to a court – practising our shots and playing around. Perhaps it had something to do with the court layout. Because tennis courts are so big, clubs tend to dot them all around the club grounds. There's rarely a focal point from where you can view all the matches at once. Squash, on the other hand, has smaller courts, normally built all in a row. Clubs often build the club bar nearby so that spectators can congregate while they watch the matches. Squash always made me feel welcome in a way that tennis didn't.

And the working life that squash has given me is astonishing. So many opportunities to meet amazing people and visit amazing places. Whenever I have a bad day and get fed up of chasing that little black ball around the court, I'm comforted to remember this.

There are currently close to 700 people on this planet playing professional squash – around 450 men and 250 women. It makes me immensely proud that, at the time of writing, I am among the top four out of all of them. In 2011 I was the best. That's what makes this sport worth playing. Not the money. The money has nothing to do with it. That's just wages.

CHAPTER 16

Eight Malaysian prostitutes

In which our hero takes on more ladies than he can handle, very nearly falls foul of Belgian police, loses a pair of his trousers in the Indian Ocean, gets punched by a Swede and wakes to find his roommate has soiled the hotel bathroom.

Quite how I ended up with a taxi full of eight very keen prostitutes, I'm not quite sure. It was Malaysia, in the early 2000s, not long after I first embarked on the professional tour. I was quite a rookie, to say the least, both in terms of squash and ladies of the night.

As were the other players with me, Adrian Grant and Adam Stevenson. On our first night in Malaysia we had some spare time to sample the Kuala Lumpur nightlife. So we rang for a taxi cab which picked us up from the hotel. The driver was a very likeable chap. After he dropped us off he gave me his business card and, winking, told me to call him if I ever needed anything.

Something obviously got lost in translation because the following evening after we phoned him up asking him to drive us into town for dinner, he turned up with no less than eight local prostitutes in the back of his cab. Yes, eight. And it was a small cab.

My boys and I were shell-shocked. First of all, how the hell do you fit eight women in the back of a small car? Secondly, what they hell were we supposed to do with them? The driver wasn't too happy when we apologised for the misunderstanding and shooed them all away. If I'd been a real man I suppose I would have offered to look after all eight myself.

That Malaysian trip was quite an eye-opener, I can tell you. The same week, after a tough match, I asked the hotel to recommend somewhere to get a massage. They obliged and I hobbled off to a local parlour where a rather butch-looking woman proceeded to throw me about her massage couch with all the bedside manner of a battlefield surgeon. There was this strange metal bar hanging above the couch, parallel with the ceiling. I discovered what it was for when she suddenly grabbed hold of it for balance while she placed the full weight of her corpulent frame onto my back. Not your regular massage. Things got seriously surreal when she terminated our meeting by asking me if I required a happy ending. (I didn't, by the way.)

When you give a bunch of 18-year-olds passports and tournament appointments in some of the world's more glamorous cities, things risk getting a little out of hand. As junior players, we certainly travelled a fair bit but we were almost always chaperoned by parents or coaches. Once you hit the adult tour, though, you are left to your own devices. And that means, if you are knocked out of a tournament early, there is the temptation of alcohol and nightlife.

Don't get me wrong. Professional squash players are not a bunch of piss artists. In the weeks before and the days during competition, we live like monks, with diet and training regimes which I guarantee are more disciplined than in most other professional sports. The bad behaviour starts once you've been knocked out. Imagine your flight doesn't go home for three more days, and the cheap airline ticket you've booked is non-exchangeable. The following week might be a week off. Naturally you're going to want to let your hair down, just like 9-to-5 office workers on a Friday night. I can't lie and say that we squash pros don't occasionally indulge in well-timed binges. And if you're thinking "What goes on tour, stays on tour", then you can think again.

In the old days, the minute the squash season had ended, Adrian Grant and I would always go on a week-long bender, normally in Leeds or Sheffield. One year I remember trying to negotiate entry to a nightclub after five nights in a row of boozing. By that stage we'd run out of clean clothes. We turned up in our hoodies with grotty T-shirts underneath. We looked and smelt like tramps. Not surprisingly, the bouncer told us to get lost.

Another time, Adrian ended up sleeping in the boot of my mum's car. We'd been out for another rather large evening and, heading back in the early hours to stay at my parents' house, we got separated. I duly crashed out, incommunicado since my phone battery had died. When Adrian turned up later I had somehow locked him out of the house. Not wanting to wake my parents, he initially tried the bed and breakfast across the street. £60 was a bit steep for a room at 3 o'clock in the morning so he found the next best option: an open car boot. My mum's open car boot, to be precise. This was the middle of winter, so when he shivered his way into the house the following morning it looked like he'd spent the night at the North Pole. Fortunately he'd woken up before my mum had left for work. She would have had quite a shock if she'd opened the boot to find him sleeping inside.

The most drunk I've ever been – and I'm not particularly proud of this – was during the European Championships in Belgium in 2009. It was the last tournament of the season. Adrian, Peter Barker and I were ready to let off some serious steam. All three of us had play-off matches the following day – mine was for third or fourth place – but by that stage we no longer cared about the outcome. As far as we were concerned, the season was already over. Without a cushioning of food inside of us (always a mistake), we set off into a town called Herentals, wondering where the hell all the locals were. It was like a ghost town. Eventually we settled into a bar for a few pints of that rather strong Belgian beer called Duvel. Everyone else, apparently, had headed off to a big party in a nearby town. We of course decided to follow suit.

On arrival we discovered a scene of utter chaos. There were thousands of revellers in a huge field in the middle of nowhere – more of a rave than a party. The only drinks available were pre-mixed cocktails and shots. I've no idea how many vodka Red Bulls and shots of sambuca we chugged down us but we somehow managed to stumble home. It was only the following morning that the other squash boys told me my behaviour had got so out of hand that I'd had a brush with the local law and very nearly spent the night in a police cell. Not clever. It's now a running joke that whenever we go on a night out another player will always offer to buy me a glass of Duvel.

Funnily enough, I didn't make it to my third/fourth place play-off the following day. My hangover (and accompanying shame) knocked the stuffing out of me completely. I was impressed with

Pete and Adrian, though. Neither of them won but they did the team proud by completing their matches. Just watching them play made my hangover feel even worse.

Pete was my roommate that week, the poor bloke. On more than one occasion he has had to tolerate drunken misbehaviour from me. I once shared a room with him in Qatar and, in a drunken haze, decided it would be a good idea to throw all of his toiletries out of the window into the hotel swimming pool. This was moments after I'd entered the hotel lobby by lying down on the conveyor belt and passing headfirst through the security X-ray machine (just like the ones you get at airports). I was lucky not to give myself brain damage.

It's not just squash players who love to let their hair down. The BBC Sports Personality of the Year after-show party is always a pretty alcohol-soaked affair. 2012 was extra soaked since it was an Olympic year. Picture the scene: athletes from every sport you can imagine, on holiday for Christmas after a year of serious hard graft, plus the added benefit of a free bar and no journalists to report on their shenanigans. Bingo. It was quite astounding to see so many dedicated athletes letting loose. Some of them were absolutely steaming drunk. I personally managed to stay up drinking until 7am, outlasting the award winner Bradley Wiggins in the process. For me, 7am is a serious achievement. I was so knackered the following morning that I missed my train home to Sheffield.

Juvenile behaviour takes place on the squash tour, just as it does in every other sport. I heard a great story from the Hong Kong Open one year when the English player Simon Parke and his mate, Canadian player Graham Ryding, decided it would be clever to test their post-drinking coordination by running down a street on top of all the parked cars. Some local heavies spotted them at their little prank and weren't too amused. Simon managed to leg it but Graham wasn't quick enough. It then turned out that one of the cars whose roofs they'd demolished belonged to a local Triad gang. When said gangsters collared Simon at his hotel the following day and threatened to break his playing arm, he immediately coughed up for the damage. A wise move, I would guess.

Exhibition tournaments offer irresistible opportunities for party time. There are no points at stake and your pay cheque is guaranteed, win or lose. In the summer of 2005 I was lucky enough to be invited out for an exhibition event on the Indian Ocean island of Reunion – the stomping ground of top French player Thierry Lincou. I was staying in a hotel with Gregory Gaultier and Renan Lavigne while Thierry was at his parents' house. So, on the final night, while the rest of us hit the island's bars, Thierry joined us late after dinner with his mum and dad. He had nothing with him but his squash kit so I lent him some trousers, a brand new pair I was rather fond of. Then we encouraged him to catch up with our drinking. Someone (I hope it wasn't me) suggested a drinking game. Since it was Thierry's home island, we felt he ought to consume the lion's share of alcohol. Of course, as with all great drinking games, the more you mess up, the more you have to drink; and the more you drink, the more you mess up. It's a vicious and cruel circle. Let's put it this way, those trousers I lent Thierry were no longer fit for purpose by the end of the evening. I happily left them behind in Reunion.

I've certainly been in a few scrapes with my good friend Adrian Grant over the years. On our first trip to Hong Kong back in 2001, when we shared a hotel room, little did we know we'd end up facing each other in the last qualifying round. The night before that match we decided to go for a little stroll around Wan Chai, one of the seedier parts of town. Young and naive, somehow we found ourselves in one of the lap-dancing joints. Since neither of us had sufficient money (you never do in those types of places), I drew the short straw and had to nip back to the hotel for my credit card. So keen was I to experience the joys of lap dancing that I sprinted all the way there and back – a good mile and a half – in Hong Kong's humid August heat. Dance complete, when we eventually left the club we spotted the England national coaches DP and Paul Carter coming out of a restaurant just down the street. Of course we hid down an alleyway until they had passed us by. We were like little kids in a sweet shop that year.

One of the better tournaments is the Swedish Open in Linkoping, run by the effervescent former pro Fredrik Johnson. On the Saturday night Freddy always organises a great party for all the players. In more recent years I've made it through to the final on the Sunday so I've made sure I'm tucked up in bed nice and early. But in 2002 I made the mistake of staying out way past my bedtime. The restaurant we were in had transformed into a nightclub and everyone had downed a few too many drinks. When some of the squash guys decided to chat up the Swedish girls, the local males took exception. As usual my big mouth got in the way when all I was trying to do was stick up for my mates. This is the only time (so far) in my life that I've been punched. And it hurt. I hit the deck but scrambled to my feet just in time to dodge the volleys of blows aimed in my direction. I got back to my hotel in record time.

The most drunk I've ever seen a squash pro (excluding myself in Herentals) was at the European Team Championships in 2005. I won't reveal the player's name since, if I did, he would never speak to me again. Unfortunately I had to share a hotel room with him. The following morning, as I was brushing my teeth, I couldn't work out why the bathroom smelt so appalling. Until I peered with trepidation into the bathtub. My roommate had got so annihilated that he'd forgotten about the toilet altogether and had fully relieved himself in the bath.

CHAPTER 17

Skulduggery

In which Nick recalls matches involving headbutts,
spitting and GBH. And how he managed to rattle
Jonathon Power with nasty aromas.

Headbutting. It's hardly the kind of behaviour you expect during a squash match. So imagine the furore at the British Open back in 1994 when Pakistani player Mir Zaman Gul planted his forehead squarely on the nose of his Australian opponent Anthony Hill. It was squash's Zinedine Zidane moment.

The incident happened just as Hill took a 7-0 lead in the final game. He clenched his fist and shouted out in triumph, all of which wound up Mir Zaman so much that he threw his racket at Hill, strode up to him and delivered his now infamous headbutt.

Immediately disqualified, the Pakistani player later said in his defence that Hill had made comments sullying his mother's reputation. Perhaps the headbutt was deserved. Who knows?

Mir Zaman had always been a bit too hot-headed for his own good, though. In 2006 he was eventually banned from the sport for life after threatening a World Squash Federation official. As for Hill, well he ended up moving to Egypt, marrying an Egyptian, converting to Islam and changing his name to Mohammed. Odd how things turn out, isn't it?

Over the years there have been dozens of outrageous incidents of sledging, cheating and fighting on the squash court. DP always reminds me of a National League match – I think it was in the 1980s – when one player kept whacking his opponent in the shins with his racket whenever the ref wasn't looking. "Have summa that!" he shouted each time he connected.

In the 1990s I remember watching a great match (I won't tell you which players) that featured lengthy rallies down the backhand wall during which one player constantly spat in his opponent's hair every time he played a shot. Disgusting but hilarious.

Not that I'm advocating cheating or violence. Far from it. However, sometimes I do think modern PSA players are far too chummy. Every time one player executes a great shot, his opponent taps him on the bum to applaud him. What's that all about? We're the best squash players in the world. We're supposed to play amazing shots. We're supposed to be busting our guts, trying to beat our opponents, not constantly reminding them how good they are. I can understand players being friendly – we spend so much time together on tour that we all develop close friendships. When you step on court, however, you need to place that friendship to one side. After all, you and your opponent both want the same thing: to win the match. You can be friends again afterwards.

What I want to know is where has all the passion, the fire and the fight gone from professional squash? Spectators don't want to see us being all cute and friendly – they want a bit of skulduggery, don't they? A bit of jiggery-pokery. Back when I first started on the PSA tour things were very different. The senior Australian players used to snarl at you if you came anywhere near them, never mind ask them for a practice hit. It was a dog-eat-dog world back then. If you were the young upstart you would very rapidly be brought back down to earth. You had to earn respect from the other players. I remember once playing John White and him telling me to "play the f***ing ball" any time I asked for a let. In contrast, nowadays players tend to be far too nice to one another. One possible exception might be Omar Mosaad, who usually walks off court in the middle of the warm-up, leaving you to hit the ball all by yourself.

It always surprises people when they learn that Gregory Gaultier is one of my best friends on tour since, whenever we play, there are always a few fireworks. He has this annoying habit of sticking his leg out and taking up too much space when he plays the ball. Some might see it as outside of the rules – blocking, in fact – while others might consider it perfectly legal. Either way it's something I just have to deal with. Any player who leaves the ball in the middle of the court deserves to be punished. As long as he doesn't tap me on

No pain, no gain. A deserted gym at Williams College
at 7am depicts the rarely seen lonely side of the sport.

Alister Walker and me at the Nürburgring. Jenson Button
and Lewis Hamilton eat your hearts out.

In the absence of the Olympics, the Commonwealth Games gives squash the biggest opportunity to shine. This is the one I would forsake all other medals to win.

The doubles double. Sharing a special moment with Adrian in Delhi. Doubles squash might not be the best spectacle, but it was my second gold so I didn't care.

Receiving my first World Open trophy in Saudi in 2010 from Ziad Al Turki, one of squash's biggest and most influential backers.

A dejected Gregory Gaultier looks on as I successfully defend my World Open title in Rotterdam in 2011. It was Greg's third defeat in a World Open final.

Playing to the 'eight corners' of the court in the British Open final against Ramy Ashour in 2012. It was probably the best performance of my career.

An outpouring of passion and emotion after reclaiming the world No.1 ranking with victory over James in the Tournament of Champions in 2012.

I have a temper on me at times.

Getting carried away after beating Greg in the World Teams in France in 2013. I love the contrast of emotions on the opposing benches. Campbell would be impressed that I can still jump this high after a torturous 138 minutes, the longest match of my career.

After a record-breaking fifth national title. With (from left) Paul Walters, my dad, DP, Auntie Sue, my mum, Esme and Neil.

Taking in the beautiful scenery at Derwent Reservoir just outside Sheffield.
And that's just my wife I'm talking about.

The emotion I felt on my wedding day made any squash
match pale into insignificance.

the bum at the end of the point. Sometimes you have to fight fire with fire. But as much as Greg and I may antagonise each other on the court, an hour or so after play, our friendship always recovers. As I always try to remember: it's just a squash match.

Sparks often fly when an Englishman finds himself on court against an Egyptian. With both countries currently dominating the top of the world rankings, there's this sense, even in individual events, that the whole pride of a nation is at stake. In the 1990s and 1980s it was much the same whenever an Australian took on a Pakistani. The great thing about these kinds of international rivalries is that they really engage the fans.

Personal rivalries get spectators excited, too. Take James Willstrop and me, for example. There's no love lost between us on the court, with every match we play guaranteed to have a bit of verbal fisticuffs. Can you imagine how dull it would be if we were best mates, always applauding each other? I think the antagonism between James and me has given British squash a much needed spicing up. Fans love it. It sells tickets.

Aside from James and Greg, I've enjoyed plenty of feisty incidents over the years. I don't do it on purpose – it's just the type of player I am. Some of the best ones have been with Jonathon Power. I think the most contentious match we ever played was our US Open quarter-final in 2005. I'll never forget what happened. He was leading two games to one, and we were halfway through the fourth game. You know the areas high on the side walls, at the back of the court, where we players tend to wipe the sweat off our hands between points? Well, I hit a serve to Jonathon that landed right on this area, so that the ball skidded as it came off the greasy wall.

Jonathon, who missed the return, was incensed, instantly accusing me of deliberately wetting the ball with sweat from my hands before serving. "What are you doing! What kind of crap is that!?" he yelled in his distinctive Canadian accent. He then exclaimed something which initially I failed to understand. "Matthew just Darwished me!" (Apparently he thought Egyptian player Karim Darwish was a bit of a ball tamperer and he was trying to place me in the same category. But you can look at the replays and see that I was innocent of all tampering.)

The match descended into farce after that. We squared up to one another, there was loads of blocking from both of us, and the bad blood was quite evident for all to see.

In the end Jonathon had to pull out halfway through the fifth game when he succumbed to serious cramp in the thumb on his playing hand. I know I shouldn't have laughed but I found the whole episode extremely funny. There he was, trying to shake hands at the end of the match, but unable to extend his hand because of the severe cramp. He obviously didn't want to look like a sore loser so he tried to straighten out his thumb by pushing it hard against the wall of the court. But to no avail. Finally he put his thumb in his mouth, determined to get rid of the cramp by biting it. Personally, I think the whole thing was slightly melodramatic. Eventually he used his left hand to shake hands with me and walked off the court.

There was an even funnier incident six years earlier, again with Jonathon Power. It was at the old Al-Ahram World Open, that wonderful tournament at the Egyptian pyramids. It was 1999 and I had qualified for the first time. Being a bit of a rookie, I'd availed myself of the local food. Big mistake. I'd had dodgy bowels all day. During the opening game against Jonathon, I was forced to release the pressure, if you know what I mean, and I'll admit the olfactory results were distinctly unpleasant, as they tend to be when food poisoning has occurred. Especially for Jonathon, on the receiving end.

Suddenly he stopped mid-rally, demanding a let. "Hang on," I thought to myself. "You can't claim a let just because someone has farted." Jonathon was adamant. He told me I'd better accept the let otherwise he would tell the ref the real reason he'd stopped playing. So I called his bluff. How exactly was he going to explain to the ref that bad smell had stopped play?

"Matthew farted, man!" he suddenly blurted out, much to the amusement of the spectators. I of course denied everything. It was pretty much a case of "He who smelt it dealt it", as far as I was concerned. Fortunately the ref took my side and refused to award a let. Perhaps, from his position outside the court, he hadn't managed to catch a whiff of my contribution – although I'm convinced it was strong enough to wake the pharaohs. In any case, I felt not a jot of guilt. There's nothing in the rules of squash saying you're not allowed to break wind.

CHAPTER 18

Let's rumble

In which brave Nick winds up a Danish tennis player, trains to Finnish dance music and messes with the Zohan.

If you're ever wondering whether a professional squash player spends a lot of time training, then know this: for every hour that you're working at your job, I am either on court practising, in the gym working out, or somewhere around the world competing. My training regime is brutal. It hurts. But the weird thing is, I sort of enjoy the pain. Besides, I know I have to go through with it if I want to continue to be successful.

As you know, my dad was a PE teacher at my school, which inevitably meant many afternoons of cross-country running. This early grounding in fitness put me in great stead for my life as a professional sportsman.

My dad knew exactly what he was doing. Even though I was years away from being a pro player, he was pretty serious about my training methods. He wanted me to be the fittest player in the club, in the region, in the country. He used to tell me he wanted my opponents to be crawling off the court at the end of matches. Whenever I complained I was tired, he would remind me of how my opponent must be feeling.

In the summer holidays we would head out to the athletics track at my school to do sprints and shuttle runs. Then he'd drag me into the gym for rigorous weight training. We'd always end with some cricket throw-downs or a kick around at football. I suppose his thinking was that he wanted the training sessions to finish on a fun note.

For two weeks every summer, the family holiday would involve travelling to the Club La Santa sports resort in Lanzarote, in the Canary Islands. Anyone who has been there will know it is the sports enthusiast's dream location. The facilities included an Olympic-sized swimming pool, athletics track, football pitch, tennis, badminton and squash courts and a full-blown gymnasium. Athletes Linford Christie and Colin Jackson once used it as their warm-weather training base. We once met boxer Frank Bruno there when he was training for one of his fights.

While on holiday at Club La Santa there were competitions organised for us for every sport under the sun. The club used to operate three skill levels: green for beginners, blue for intermediates, and red for advanced. By that stage my squash was already pretty advanced so I would always enter the adult red squash tournament… and usually win it. The vanquished grown-ups were so incredulous they'd lost to a pre-pubescent kid that they'd usually challenge me to a rematch the following morning. I'd then beat them all over again.

One year, when I lost in the tournament final, I was so distraught that, for once, it was me who challenged my opponent to a rematch the next morning. I got my revenge. The fact that he'd been in the resort nightclub until about seven o'clock in the morning didn't make my victory any less sweet.

I remember frustrating a few blokes in the blue tennis tournament, too. In the years since I'd given up tennis, my topspin forehand had completely deteriorated so I decided to slice the ball on both sides using a big squash swing. One day it was so windy that my sliced drop shot landed on my opponent's side of the net and then spun back onto my side of the court. The Danish fellow I was playing was incensed, storming off the court, yelling "This is just not tennis!"

Once a week the club would organise a ceremony where all the winners from the past seven days would receive their certificates. More often than not, accompanying us at Club La Santa were my parents' best friends Pete and Jan, and their sons Tom and Paul. Between us all there was always a competition to see who could win the most club certificates. We'd pin them all up on the wall of our shared apartment and take turns gloating. Pete was something of a cheat, entering the green events for all the sports in his greed to win as many certificates as possible. He was particularly strong in the golf putting competition. Tom was a handy squash player himself, a Durham & Cleveland county junior. One week he talked me into not entering the squash tournament so he could have a crack at the title and then proceeded to get knocked out in the first round. Tom and I had a superb record in the pool tournament, though. I think we must have won it eight times. The prize each time was a bottle of champagne which, since we were under age, my dad and Pete would happily guzzle for us.

***

By the time I reached 17, I was training for the World Junior Championships. My dad rightly felt I needed to put in the hours at lunchtime and after school. Lunchtime meant training on the school playing fields. You can imagine the reaction I got from other kids. "Faster, you fat git! Faster!" they would shout encouragingly while munching on their sweets and crisps. When my dad was out of earshot, their words of exhortation were a little ruder.

Once a week I would catch the train down to Nottingham to play against some of the top senior professionals based there. There was a great stable of players there at the time: Simon Parke, Alex Gough, Derek Ryan, John White – all had been ranked in the world top 10 at one time or another. But the guy I most often played against was Peter Marshall. As I explained earlier, Peter was recovering after several years out of the game with chronic fatigue syndrome. Before his illness he had enjoyed the reputation of being one of the fittest players the squash world had ever seen. He'd reached No.2 in the world and was the closest challenger to the great Jansher Khan.

I always knew where I stood with Peter. I'd only win a point off him if I'd truly earned it. He had this relentless style and, despite all those lunchtime fitness sessions with my dad at school, I was usually knackered after about five points. I found his unique double-handed style impossible to read. In almost every rally he would send me the wrong way. The first time I went to Nottingham, I finished the day trudging back to the train station, having received a painful 9-0, 9-0, 9-0 thrashing. After that I went down every week for further punishment. On the second occasion I won one point, the third time three points, and then, the week before leaving for the World Junior Championships, I won six points in the first game alone. I was improving. I thought perhaps Peter was being nice to me in order to build up my confidence but that really wasn't his style. His philosophy was: if you get anything for free, you'll never learn how hard you need to work. Nowadays, every time I have a game with a young player, I try to apply the same philosophy.

***

As I edged ever closer to the professional game, my dad realised I needed more specific and more expert training advice. He had recently read an article in the British Journal of Sports Medicine by an expert in the field called Edward Winter. Ed worked out of one of De Montfort University's campuses in Bedford, which is where he first subjected me to a fitness test. The test was overseen by the aforementioned Damon Leedale-Brown. It was my first experience of being wired up and poked and prodded like a guinea pig. My left index finger was sore the next day from the numerous blood samples they took. As well as being a fitness expert, Damon was also a strong squash player himself so his advice in strength, conditioning and nutrition was invaluable. For me, this was the most sophisticated physical training I'd ever witnessed.

Less than two years after that initial test, by an incredible stroke of luck, Ed and Damon relocated to Sheffield's Hallam University, just down the road from me. I had just turned professional so the timing couldn't have been better. It meant I could benefit from Damon's training sessions three or four times a week. We did weights in the university gym and on-court training at my club. I remember each time Damon turned up, the boot of his car looked like he'd just raided a circus props department: ladders, cones, Swiss balls, medicine balls, hula hoops, therabands. There was enough stuff in there for any number of clowns or trapeze acts. Much to his dismay, whenever he opened up the boot I'd say: "Looks like the circus is in town."

Anyone who's ever done serious fitness training will know about something called the bleep test. For those of you uninitiated, it basically involves running shuttle runs progressively faster between two cones, ensuring that you complete each shuttle before the next bleep sounds. Damon came up with this brilliant idea for a bleep test specific to squash. Instead of doing shuttle runs, I would do ghosting movements instead. But I still had to complete a set number of movements before each bleep sounded. Over the years, two bleep tests have developed. One is a total speed version in which you have to complete one lap of the test as fast as humanly possible. The other is a repeated speed version where you have to keep a consistent pace over a high number of reps. These are still the standard tests for squash players of all ages on the England national squad.

Damon used to set me killer bike sessions too. He would make me a MiniDisc (Yes, it was that long ago that we listened to music on the now obselete MiniDisc) with music that would speed up and slow down depending on the difficulty of the training session. Whenever Sandstorm by Darude came on – a very fast, upbeat Finnish dance track – you knew you were in trouble.

In 2003 the English Institute of Sport opened in Sheffield and, thanks to my Lottery funding, I was given full use of it. On site were doctors, physios, psychologists, nutritionists, massage therapists and strength and conditioning coaches. I was so lucky to have such an amazing facility right on my doorstep.

Around this time I switched to a trainer called Tommy Yule, a former Commonwealth Games medallist in weight-lifting. Tommy had no prior knowledge of squash but he knew exactly how to make a sportsman powerful. That guy was seriously strong. He was the first person to introduce me to dynamic exercises known as plyometrics. These involve using maximum force in minimum time – so lots of explosive jumping, leaping and bounding.

During my younger years I had developed a good physical engine (in part thanks to my cross-country running at school) and, through Damon, a good base of strength. But to compete at the top level I needed more speed and power. So under Tommy I started doing heavier squat exercises in the gym but with lower numbers of reps. Instead of resting in between sets of squats I would do a series of plyometric exercises. It was a great way to get my legs moving powerfully when they were already fatigued. To work on my agility

Tommy then had me chasing a reaction ball (one of those rubber things with loads of knobs sticking out of it) around the gym like Rocky Balboa chasing the chicken. I'll never forget how he always had this massive bunch of keys jangling from his belt. In order to become more explosive off the mark – an essential skill in a sport like squash – Tommy used to get me doing short, 10-metre sprints. He was so fast he would beat me every time over this distance, even when I was warmed up in my running kit and he was still cold with all those keys jangling from his belt. Thanks to Tommy, my strength and power came on in leaps and bounds. I owe him an enormous debt.

In 2007 I met my third serious trainer, Mark Campbell. A cross between Damon and Tommy, he came from a rugby union background. But he had a deep knowledge of squash thanks to his years as a club-level player. If you need proof of his expertise in the physical side of the sport, just look at the roster of players he was training as I wrote this book: me, James Willstrop, Adrian Grant, Alister Walker and Madeline Perry.

It wasn't long before my shoulder operation that I first teamed up with Mark, so one of his early challenges was to keep me sane by devising an exercise regime during my long recuperation. That's when he invented the strength and conditioning circuits that have since become so infamous within the world of squash: we call them The Rumble.

The Rumble is absolute torture. There's no other way of describing it. And it's my fault that Mark first devised it. We were enjoying a game of snooker one day and I happened to show him a copy of Men's Health magazine with a feature on my good self in it. There was another article in the magazine that caught Mark's eye all about a fitness sport called CrossFit. Practised at gyms all over the world, CrossFit is a combination of weight-lifting, gymnastics, aerobic exercises and exercises using just your own body weight. It's massive out in the States but it's getting very popular in Europe too.

Mark enjoys the pain of tough training and will regularly join in with the sessions he sets us. This new CrossFit thing was something he just couldn't resist. He had soon signed up for a CrossFit event, and he loved it, so he decided to use his experience to create a similar all-body workout which we eventually called The Rumble.

The problem with training for squash is that you need to be something of an all-rounder. You need both speed and stamina. You need flexibility but also strength. You need technical proficiency but also mental fortitude. The list goes on. It's impossible to train all of these aspects all of the time. Out of all the off-court sessions I've ever done, The Rumble is the one that ticks most of these boxes. And that's why, now, when I'm not at a tournament, I spend at least seven days a month doing repeated lunges, medicine ball throws, sprints, skipping, sled-dragging, step exercises and dumbbell press-ups. Utter physical punishment.

It's vastly different from how squash training used to be. I used to hear stories about Jonah Barrington and Geoff Hunt's training regimes. Their off-court sessions involved brutal sets of 400-metre sprints which seemed to match the physical requirements of the sport at the time. The modern game has glass courts, a lower tin, technologically advanced rackets and a different scoring system, all of which can make for shorter and more explosive rallies. The Rumble prepares you much better for these types of rallies. It's a full body workout done at dynamic intervals with very little rest. Much like a game of squash. A typical Rumble session lasts non-stop for between 40 and 60 minutes with the only rest being the time it takes to walk from one exercise station to the next. Sometimes Mark will keep me on my toes by demanding a shorter Rumble at the end of an easier physical session. Those short Rumbles might last only three or four minutes but even that can make you feel like puking. Imagine how brutal the full-length ones are.

The Rumble has become legendary within squash circles. Whenever a player comes up to train with me for a few days we always challenge them to one. We crank up the music and get lots of banter going between the different players. There's often a T-shirt prize at stake. It all stems from Ian Pyper, Mark's assistant, who decided to join in one day. It was a particularly brutal Rumble on that occasion and he eventually came to a standstill during the sled-dragging sprints. After that he became famous as the man who got broken by The Rumble. The next time Ian turned up to the gym he brought with him a T-shirt he'd found at home with the word 'Unbreakable' on the front of it. Now, whoever performs best during The Rumble gets to keep the T-shirt and wear it during the next session when everyone else tries to win it back – a bit like a tournament trophy but a lot, lot sweatier.

Men's Health magazine even got to hear about The Rumble and ran a feature on it a couple of years ago.

***

Every summer I head off to Williams College (an American university in Williamstown, Massachusetts) for a fortnight of warm-weather training. Mark always makes sure I have a strict training programme. He certainly has plenty of options since the facilities there are superb. In general, American universities make the British equivalents pale into insignificance.

This fortnight is probably my best training period of the entire year. Williamstown is such a quiet part of the world with no distractions at all. Apart from a few hours of coaching that I do with the junior camps every morning (which pays for us to be there), I have the rest of the day to focus on my training. It's what I call "sleep, eat, train, repeat". A typical day starts at 7am with cardio work in the gym or on the running track from 7.15am to 8.15am. After breakfast I then coach the camps from 9am until midday. Lunch is followed by an afternoon nap – by far the best part of the day. Then, around 3pm, I get in the swimming pool or do a weights session followed by an hour on court at 4pm and sometimes back to the running track for some short sprints. Busy days, indeed, but I love them. Either Neil or DP will travel out there with me and there will be a few younger professional players to keep me on my toes. With temperatures well above 30 degrees every day, it gets my body used to the heat.

The junior camps are run through a company called Squash and Beyond by a good friend of mine Zafi Levy. Originally from Israel, Zafi was a student at Williams and is now their director of squash. He's a loveable rogue. If you've ever seen the movie You Don't Mess with the Zohan, starring Adam Sandler, then you'll know the type. Zafi is just like the Zohan. He's one of the few people I've ever met who's more competitive than I am. Because of this, every year we have a good-natured falling out on the football pitch and on the golf course. I tease him that he has a habit of dropping a new golf ball down his trouser leg if he can't find his ball.

He does a brilliant job on the junior camps, though. They operate for ten weeks throughout the summer with different professional players or coaches taking turns to help for a fortnight each. With over 40 kids per week, the camps are always fully booked, proof that squash is growing in America, especially on the East Coast. However, none of the kids are interested in becoming a professional player. What they're aiming for is to improve their squash to such a level that they're able to win a scholarship to a good university. This in itself is great. As long as the kids enjoy playing squash, I'm happy. But I'd love it if, one day in the future, there was an American player at the top of the world rankings. If squash were ever to grow truly big in America, it would do wonders for the sport worldwide.

***

The best physical training sessions are without doubt those you do with other athletes. You need another squash man in the gym or on the track to give you a boost when you're starting to tire, and to create a bit of rivalry. Adrian Grant was my first serious training partner. When he was 18 he moved from London to Yorkshire. He told me he was getting into too much trouble down south in the capital. So when he arrived he was well up for a strict training regime. For two consecutive summers, during the squash off-season, we would get up every day at 7am and do long, hard runs around The Stray, this huge, 200-acre park right in the middle of Harrogate.

We were living together in a place known as 'The Squash House', a property that DP used to rent out at bargain rates to squash players. Every morning, as Adrian and I came back from our early runs, the other players were just starting to emerge from their beds. It gave us a physical and a psychological boost to know that we had already completed a training session before our housemates were even awake.

Then we'd head for the squash club (Harrogate Squash & Fitness Centre), do solo practices, a group session and finally a one-on-one session with DP. We did loads of ghosting and sprinting sessions on court in the afternoon. I still have nightmares about those shuttle sprints we did: up and down 10 times, short rest. Up and down 20 times, short rest. Up and down 30 times, short rest. That continued until you'd done 50 shuttles. Then you worked your way back down in increments of 10. I suffered from back problems at that time so by the second half of the session my back muscles would start to go into spasm.

My second training partner was a chap called Bradley Ball who reached the top 30 of the world rankings. Bradley was from Ipswich and used to come up to Sheffield to train for a week at a time. His training methods were a little suspect, however. All he ever wanted to do was play matches or do squats. I'd beg him to do drills or gym sessions but he'd always say, "No, I just want to play." During his week's stay we'd play up to 10 times.

We called him Brad Attack because we'd never seen anyone hit the ball as hard on the backhand as he could. And he'd aim for the nick on just about every shot. He certainly used to keep me on my toes, giving me some real humdingers of matches, often stretching to the high teens in the fifth game. They may have been friendly matches but either of us would have died rather than lose. Other club members at Hallamshire used to get really annoyed because we'd always end up playing on beyond our allotted court time.

Eventually I managed to lure Bradley into the gym for some proper training. So while he beat me up on the court, I would, in turn, try to beat him up with the workouts. It was a good combination.

Apart from that blistering backhand, the two things I remember most about Bradley were his claw-shaped feet – we all joked that he used to perch upside down at night like a bat – and his appalling diet. Some days he seemed to live on just a handful of bananas and energy bars. He wasn't the most patient of guys either, hence his all-action playing style. Once, in Sheffield, he got lost while driving to the English Institute of Sport and became so frustrated that, seeing a sign for the M1, he decided to drive home to Ipswich instead. So rather than a local journey, he had a 175-mile slog all the way from Yorkshire to East Anglia. That's how impatient he was.

In 2007 I started training with Alister Walker. It was just after I had met Mark Campbell, who really encouraged both of us to push each other to our physical limits. On one hurdle session I remember us being so competitive that I nearly bust my cruciate ligament, cracking my knee on the top of a hurdle. It was during this time, just before my shoulder operation, that I trained harder than I had ever done before. One session in particular, in which Alister and I lifted our maximum weights on the squat exercise and then did sprints on the running track, will live long in my memory. Afterwards, both of us were so physically drained that we couldn't speak for half an hour. That's very unusual for a motormouth like me.

I pride myself on my fitness but Alister did one session with Mark that beggared belief, even for me. They ran 100 metres 100 times with less than a minute's rest between each run. I can tell you I was very glad to be away at a tournament for that session.

Because I was higher-ranked, other players used to view Alister as my protégé, rather than as an equal. I always thought that was very insulting to him since he was a highly talented up-and-coming player at the time. During our time training together, he rose from No.40 in the world to No.12.

In all sports there comes a time when two training partners cease to benefit from each other. Perhaps they run out of ideas. Perhaps they get too accustomed to each other's playing style. Like in an emotional relationship, perhaps the spark disappears. During the 2012 Olympics I was watching Michael Johnson discussing some of the sprinters. He certainly knows his stuff, Michael Johnson does. He was talking about how, back in 2000, the Olympic champion Maurice Greene had been training with his main rival Ato Boldon. Greene was clearly the stronger of the two. Johnson suggested it was crazy that Boldon could even contemplate winning a gold medal when he was training every day with a sprinter who was faster than him. If he wanted to overtake his rival he needed a clean break.

This is often the case in squash, too. Imagine if I decided to move to Egypt and train with Ramy Ashour. It's unthinkable. To maintain our position as rivals we need to be removed from each other both physically and psychologically. I think, in the case of Alister, he knew he had to break away from me if he wanted his own game to really flourish. Sure enough, in 2010 we stopped training together.

***

Another physical aspect of squash that is absolutely crucial is physiotherapy. You've already read about how Jade Elias manipulates my body and keeps me functioning properly. I've been incredibly lucky to work with other brilliant therapists at the English Institute of Sport. For over a decade now, my massage therapist has been a guy called Derry Suter. Derry regularly has a high-class roster of meat on his massage table including the likes of Olympic heptathlete Jessica Ennis-Hill. Sessions with Derry are legendary. He must have the sharpest elbows in the entire world and takes great pleasure in screwing them into the plantar fascia on the bottom of your feet. Despite the pain, he keeps my body in one piece.

Squash players should never underestimate the importance of massage therapy. When Alister Walker first started training with us, Derry boasted that by massage alone he could get him into the world top 20. And he was right: in 2009 Alister reached No.12. Whether that was all down to Derry is of course open to debate. One thing that's for certain, however, is that Derry is one of the top therapists on the planet. In the past he has got me back on court after injury in half the time expected by the medical experts. Esme always jokes that the only person in the world that I value more than her is Derry. High praise indeed.

CHAPTER 19

Bigmouth strikes again

In which Nick analyses his Sheffield identity, praises his mum's
Yorkshire pudding and his beloved Sheffield Wednesday, and
gets embedded in a city pavement.

Can you be defined by the county you come from? I think maybe
you can when that county's Yorkshire.

I have a couple of characteristics that particularly mark me out
as a typical Yorkshireman. I'm always very blunt, very straight to
the point. I can assure you that, with me, you always know where
you stand. Often that's a positive thing. Unfortunately it also gets
me into trouble with squash referees since I tend to blurt out things
without thinking. "Subtle as a brick" is how DP describes me. I
wear my heart on my sleeve but I admit I often end up with my foot
in my mouth.

Take the 2006 US Open as a good example. I was up against
Amr Shabana in the quarter-finals in a closely fought match. In
charge of proceedings was a female referee from Canada. After a
crucial decision that didn't go my way, I stupidly vocalised what
I was thinking. I said to her: "You should be reffing the women's
tournament down the road!" The minute the words escaped from
my mouth I knew what an idiot I had been. I thought, "Oh my God!
What a crass thing to say, you utter fool!" I just wanted the court to
open up and swallow me right there and then. Quite rightly, just as
the crowd were venting their disapproval by booing me loudly, the
referee docked me a point. I later received a £500 fine.

Afterwards she was incredibly forgiving about the whole
incident. The following day when we met up for a chat I felt
horrendous, such a sexist idiot, but she was very understanding. She

said she appreciated the emotional pressure we players sometimes find ourselves under. She even (Would you believe it?) admitted that she had got the original decision wrong. It still didn't excuse my reaction, though.

I've been fined one other time in my career. That, you'll remember from an earlier chapter, was when I lost to Peter Barker in the quarter-finals in Hong Kong. I'd just reached No.1 in the world and probably felt I was a bit invincible. After smashing my racket, instead of apologising, I got into a heated argument with some of the spectators. There's no dignified way out of that kind of situation.

My big Yorkshire mouth nearly got me sent home from the 2006 Commonwealth Games. On the very first day, all the female players were told they had to attend an official function on behalf of England Squash. The male players were to attend a similar function the following week. Linda Elriani, one of the female team members, had voiced her disapproval at this. Naturally, with matches to prepare for, they were keen to get out of the engagement. I then stupidly blurted out, "Why don't you go to this function since you won't be here next week anyway?" The week before, Linda had complained to DP about being omitted from the doubles team. She had implied she wanted to fly home after the first week (doubles was during the second week) since there was no point in her staying there. In the end she stayed on to support, but I thought that her team spirit should have been stronger and I told her so. I didn't realise how sensitive she was – and just how insensitive I was – until she started crying. The England Squash performance director, a guy called Peter Hirst, with whom I already didn't see eye to eye, then found out what I'd done. After he reprimanded me, my big Yorkshire mouth stepped in once more and told him unequivocally to "Get lost!" For that little stunt he tried to get me sent home until coach DP managed to smooth things over. In private, DP told me he was pleased that I had stood up for myself (and him) but that, in reality, he couldn't condone what I had done. It's the story of my life really: I might have a valid point to make but the manner in which I make it regularly gets me into trouble.

Perhaps my character is more defined by being a Sheffielder rather than a Yorkshireman, though. Sheffielders can be a bit different to the rest of Yorkshire in that they're a bit more big-city in their outlook. Less flat caps and whippets, more steel industry and The Full Monty.

It's strange. That 1997 film, The Full Monty, is such an unflattering Sheffield cliché that I'm always reluctant to use it. However, when I find myself in some far-flung corner of the PSA tour – in Asia or South America, for example – and I try to explain to people where I hail from, the only viable point of reference is The Full Monty. You can bang on about the River Don, the Peak District, The Crucible and the Sheffield music scene as much as you like but it won't mean a thing to a Pakistani or a Colombian. Mention The Full Monty, though – a cheesy film about unemployed miners who strip naked – and their eyes light up. A bit like Seattle was defined by Frasier in the 1990s; or Boston was defined by Cheers in the 1980s; or Liverpool was defined by The Beatles in the 1960s. Except the inhabitants of those cities are perhaps prouder of Frasier, Cheers and The Beatles than we Sheffielders are of The Full Monty.

In many ways I think it's a shame that Sheffield is always so strongly associated with the steel industry. Of course we should be proud of our industrial past, but modern Sheffield has so much more to it than steel. I find that, especially in the south of England, people assume Sheffield is some sort of industrial wasteland where everyone works down a mine or makes steel and is attached to an iron lung. Believe me, there's so much more to Sheffield than that. And I've never met anyone with an iron lung.

Sheffield is actually very cosmopolitan and one of the largest cities in the UK. It's also incredibly green with over 80 parks and part of the Peak District National Park within the city boundary. I sound like I'm doing publicity for the tourism office. Actually, at this juncture I ought to declare an interest: I am an official ambassador for the Yorkshire tourist board, so I'm naturally a little biased about the delights of my region.

Joking aside, Sheffield really is very green. Apparently there are more than two million trees across the city. Out of my living room window in Totley I can see a good proportion of them. I once heard our town called "the greenest city in Europe", although that's a mighty bold claim.

It's also a very sporty city, home town for the likes of athletes Jessica Ennis-Hill and Sebastian Coe, footballer Gordon Banks, cricketer Michael Vaughan, boxers Johnny Nelson and Naseem Hamed and tennis player Roger Taylor.

The facilities for squash are brilliant and I really count myself lucky that I can live and train in my home town. I know so many other squash professionals who have had to relocate to training bases miles from where their family and friends live. Some of the Aussies, for example, have to find themselves European or American training bases simply because there are so few tournaments their side of the planet. I, on the other hand, have everything I need right here on my doorstep and I'm convinced this has helped me have a longer career than if I'd been forced to move elsewhere for squash facilities. When I come home it really is my home. You won't believe how comforting it is for me to be able to nip round to my parents' house for Sunday lunch and enjoy my mum's famous Yorkshire pudding. I know every Yorkshire lad says this but I truly believe my mum makes the greatest Yorkshire pudding known to man. It's so good that on an early date with Esme I decided to take her to my mum and dad's for a Sunday roast. I was sure the Yorkshire pud would seal the deal. (And it did!)

There are many Sheffielders who make me proud to hail from this city. Jessica Ennis-Hill is a great example. Not only because of her Olympic achievement but also because, despite all the fame, she has stuck to her roots and remained in Sheffield. (Granted, she lives in a rather bigger house nowadays.) Given her celebrity status, it wouldn't have been surprising if she'd relocated to London after the Olympics to make the most out of commercial opportunities. But, no, she's stayed here in Sheffield. She's exactly the same girl I first met over a decade ago.

Outside Sheffield's town hall there's a special tribute to the city's most famous sons and daughters. Called Sheffield Legends, it's a Hollywood Boulevard-style chain of plaques set into the pavement. Jessica's there, of course, as is Seb Coe, Gordon Banks, Michael Vaughan, the actor Sean Bean, singer Joe Cocker, the novelist Margaret Drabble, rock band Def Leppard, former Python Michael Palin and first British astronaut Helen Sharman. Guess who's a recent addition to the Sheffield Legends? Yes, yours truly. So next time you're pounding the pavements of Sheffield, have a look down and see if you can wipe your feet on my name.

Sean Bean is a Sheffielder I particularly admire. Nowadays the actor is proper Hollywood A-list – he's been in Game of Thrones, The Lord of the Rings, he was even a James Bond baddie – yet he remains loyal to his Sheffield roots. He still regularly comes back to the city, he hasn't lost his south Yorkshire accent and he's a staunchly loyal Sheffield United fan.

This brings me neatly on to football. For those of you not familiar with my city, there are two major football clubs round here, both a major part of the city's culture: Sheffield United and the glorious Sheffield Wednesday. No guesses where my loyalties lie. I have been an Owls fan (as we Wednesday supporters are known) for as long as I can remember. My dad used to take me to Hillsborough as a kid and I've followed the club's fortunes, both waxing and waning, ever since.

I remember my first ever game there: in May 1988 my mighty Owls were tonked 5-1 by a Liverpool side containing the likes of John Barnes, Peter Beardsley and Steve McMahon.

Some of my favourite sporting memories have been while watching Sheffield Wednesday's exploits. In 1991 I went down to Wembley with my dad to witness them beating Manchester United in the final of the League Cup (or the Rumbelows Cup as it was then known). It was the Easter weekend and my mum, my dad and I were booked in to see the British Open squash next door in the old Wembley Conference Centre the previous day. Imagine what a thrill for me it was. I think it might have been the best weekend of my childhood. Just 10 years old. I get to watch top-level squash on the Saturday and my football team wins the Cup on the Sunday. It was that weekend, watching the likes of Jahangir and Jansher Khan, when I first realised that I wanted to be a professional squash player.

I remember being a massive fan of Wednesday's winger Chris Waddle. He played for the club between 1992 and 1996 and always had this incredible move that he did on the wing involving a step-over dummy. He would feign crossing the ball with his right foot before, at the last split-second, he'd step inside the defender and whip the ball across with his left foot. In the old days, right-footed players would always play on the right wing and left-footed players always on the left. But Waddle was an anomaly, one of the first left-footers to play on the right wing. It used to really confuse defenders and they'd fall for his little dummy every time. You might say he made a career out of it. In 1993 Waddle won the footballer of the year award, the first player outside the top six teams to do so.

My other favourite Wednesday player was David Hirst, the club's record goal-scorer. He was so good that in 1993 Manchester Utd bid a whopping £4.5 million for him. That may sound like peanuts now but back then it was staggering. Wednesday turned it down, though, and a few months later Hirst got an injury that meant he was never again the same force on the pitch. In 2010, after I won my Commonwealth Games medals, I was invited down onto the pitch at Sheffield Wednesday where Hirst presented me with a match shirt signed by the team. A very proud moment. (For me, not him.)

As a Wednesday fan I have inevitably endured long periods of suffering, too. When I was a kid we were proudly in the top flight of English football before rapidly dropping down two divisions in the early 2000s. It wasn't our greatest period. But I loyally follow the club's fortunes, even when I'm the other side of the planet, playing squash. Every Saturday afternoon, without fail, I desperately search out internet access so I can discover what the Owls have been up to. It's a great way for me to maintain a link with my home town when I'm abroad for long periods of time. And it means I've become an utter anorak about my team, with more statistical knowledge than is healthy for me. I can tell you every Wednesday player since 1990. I have all the player and team stats engrained on my mind – what the scores were, who scored, who won awards, when we were promoted, relegated etc. Thanks to my obsession with the Owls, a lot of the other squash players have adopted them as a sort of second team.

It pains me to write this but, in recent years, I have been strongly involved with Sheffield United as well – simply because they have more club community programmes. Sheffield's other team also have links with England Squash since the club chairman, Kevin McCabe, is a passionate squash fan. He's watched loads of my matches and once himself played a pro-am match against Jonah Barrington. Any time I want to go to the directors' box at Sheffield Utd I just have to ask. (Within reason.) They also support my squash academy at Hallamshire. The Jessica Ennis-Hill stand at Bramall Lane even had an England Squash banner hanging up in it with an enormous photo of me splashed across it. Try hiding that from football fans.

Just imagine the stick I now get from Wednesday fans. The rivalry between United fans (Blades) and Wednesday fans (Owls) in this city is a bit like United and City fans in Manchester. You're born one or the other and would rather die than switch allegiance. Which puts me in a slightly awkward position. It used to be that, like all Wednesday fans, I despised Sheffield United with a vengeance. But given their support of squash, I have since mellowed with age. The club management have been really good to me so it would be churlish of me not to wish them well and hope they rejoin Wednesday in the Championship. At the time of writing they were one league below in League One.

But I will always be a Wednesday fan at heart. Nowadays I suppose I want both teams to fare well – it's part of my love of the city of Sheffield… as long as Wednesday remain above United in the league.

Despite all my great football memories, you can't talk about Sheffield Wednesday without remembering the Hillsborough disaster. All English football fans know that, in 1989, Hillsborough Stadium was the scene of one of the worst football tragedies ever when 96 Liverpool fans were crushed to death during an FA Cup semi-final. Sheffield Wednesday weren't playing that day – the stadium had been chosen as a neutral ground specially for the FA Cup match – but club fans have always felt very compassionate about the tragedy. It took place on our turf.

CHAPTER 20

Bombs, Kalashnikovs and earthquakes

In which we see our champion surviving an earthquake, avoiding the attention of trigger-happy terrorists and getting scared witless during a flight back from Malaysia.

I once slept through an earthquake. I was sharing a hotel room in the Pakistani city of Islamabad with James Willstrop during the 2005 World Team Championships. It was early in the morning and we both went down to breakfast, still a bit groggy, suddenly aware of a commotion among the other guests. We had no idea what all the fuss was about. Then it turned out that, during the night, an earthquake measuring five on the Richter scale had struck our hotel. That's by no means massive, but fairly frightening, all the same. (By comparison, the 2013 earthquake in New Zealand was 3.7 on the scale.) And we'd slept blissfully through the entire thing.

I remember thinking to myself, "Okay, that explains the bookcase knocked over onto the floor of our hotel room and the bedside lamp that had fallen over." It was a very strange experience.

It was even stranger, given that James has a reputation on the tour for being an incurable insomniac. He must have slept deeply that night since he didn't hear a squeak either.

Fortunately our hotel, the Islamabad Marriott, wasn't at the earthquake's epicentre. (That was in Kashmir where it registered at a scary 7.6 on the Richter scale.) A few days later the squash tournament we were competing at organised a hospital tour so that we could visit some of the quake victims and try to cheer them up. (Quite how a British squash pro might cheer up someone with multiple broken limbs is beyond me but we went, all the same, glad to help.) It was quite an eye opener. We met people with every conceivable part of their body damaged and bandaged. And we saw some of the worst-wrecked buildings across the city.

But it was inside our hotel that we saw the damage close-up. In countries like Pakistan, where foreigners aren't particularly encouraged to wander around the cities, hotels tend to have a whole village of shops and restaurants inside their confines; partly to make it convenient for the guests, and partly to extricate a bit of extra cash from them. Our Marriott was no exception. On the ground floor, near the reception, there were dozens of gift shops selling souvenirs, pashminas, delicacies and all the usual touristy rubbish. The blokes running these shops were the nicest, most friendly you were likely to meet. They were experienced salesmen and always trying to part you from your cash. But they had a great sense of humour. Humble, friendly shopkeepers.

I remember walking through the lobby the morning after the earthquake and surveying the damage. For a few of them it was chaos, especially the ones selling souvenirs. There were trinkets scattered all over the floor. I saw various pottery and glass gifts smashed to bits. Even though close to 80,000 people had been killed elsewhere by this earthquake, I couldn't help focusing on these cheap, mundane gifts smashed on the lobby floor. It was pathetic really. Especially when you think of all the lives that had been lost. But something about those broken trinkets really played on my mind.

I'll never forget, three years later, when I was back home at my parents' house watching the news one evening. Suddenly this report came on about a major bombing in Islamabad. I looked at the pictures and realised it was our Marriott Hotel – the one where we'd slept through the earthquake – that had been hit. A terrorist had filled a dumper truck with 1,300lbs of explosives and detonated the lot right in front of the hotel reception. The blast killed more than 50 people, destroyed much of the hotel and left a crater 20 metres wide and six metres deep. I kept thinking about those poor guys who worked in the souvenir shops and their broken souvenirs. They didn't stand a chance. They'd survived an earthquake and then, three years later, they got blown to bits by a massive terrorist bomb. The whole gruesome incident really shook me up.

It wasn't the only time I've stayed in a hotel that later became involved in a terrorist attack. The 2013 Boston Marathon bombing was a block or so away from the Lenox Hotel, on Boylston St, where I stay every year when we compete in that city. Seeing the bombing on TV made me very worried indeed.

Mumbai, in India, freaked me out a bit, too. It was November 2009 and we were playing the Punj-Lloyd PSA Masters. You have to realise that this was just a year after the Mumbai terrorist attacks and we were staying in a hotel that had been targeted: the Taj Mahal Palace Hotel. The hotel wasn't officially open to the public but the tournament organisers had managed to book us in there. They must have secured a decent rate because there was still scaffolding everywhere for the repairs to the damage from the gunfight between terrorists and Indian commandos. A total of 31 people had died in the hotel that day.

It was a strange atmosphere when we arrived. The hotel employees acted like it was business as usual but they were still making repairs to all the bullet holes in the walls. In the stairwell around the back it looked like they were actually plucking bullets from holes in the plasterwork. I remember switching on the TV in my room and on came this documentary about the same attacks a year earlier. The narrator was describing how hotel guests had locked themselves in their rooms to hide from the gunmen. It was bizarre – like being on an aeroplane and watching an airline disaster movie.

Not surprisingly, just a year on, the hotel security was beefier than ever. Any time you wanted to get back into the hotel building it took about 20 minutes to pass through the security cordon of X-ray machines and armed guards.

At the back of the hotel there was a superb swimming pool. It was absolute paradise. But I remember lying on a sun-lounger and looking at the fences between the pool and the city streets behind the hotel. They were fairly low. Anyone could have leapt over them. So while it took us 20 minutes to get through the front door, it might have taken a miscreant and his Kalashnikov just 20 seconds to vault the back fence. There I was, sunning myself, thinking that if someone really wanted to kill me there wasn't much I could do to stop them. But at the same time, in that Mumbai hotel that had been shot to smithereens the year before, I felt totally safe. Lightning never strikes the same place twice, right?

Thanks to the popularity of squash across the Middle East – in no small way due to Pakistani player Jahangir Khan's dominance throughout the 1980s – there are loads of major tournaments staged in Muslim countries. We Western players are always told by the various squash authorities that we are potential terrorist targets. The UK Home Office advises Brits not even to visit some of the more unstable areas. I've got to say, we're better off ignoring the Home Office website. The travel advice it posts on there scares the living daylights out of me sometimes. And these are countries I'm obliged to visit if I want to continue earning a living.

In fact, I ignore the travel advice so much that you might accuse me of burying my head in the sand. I have to admit that professional players tend to be a bit blasé much of the time about security. The tournaments put us up in really smart hotels and often provide armed escorts wherever we go. Even though we are competing in countries with regular terrorist incidents, we live a very sheltered existence, I suppose. From airports to hotels to tournament venues, we're in a bubble. It's not like we're wandering the back streets.

And remember that we are squash players, not cricketers or footballers. Often it's reassuring to know that squash is really low-key compared to the major world sports. If I was an international cricketer in Pakistan, for example, or a world-famous footballer, I'd be constantly worried I was going to get my head blown off by a trigger-happy terrorist. I may be one of the very best squash players on the planet, but virtually everyone outside the world of squash struggles to recognise me. I don't think your average terrorist would be able to pick me out in a crowd.

In Pakistan squash is a vastly higher-profile sport than it is in the UK. And here's a country which has had more than its fair share of terrorist attacks. Back in 2009 the PSA was forced to suspend five tournaments there over security concerns. It got to this rather bizarre situation where top players were refusing to travel to Pakistan for fear of being targeted by terrorists while lower-ranked players were willing to run the gauntlet. And I can understand why. Imagine if the whole of the world top 10 should decide to boycott an event because of terrorist risks. The world No.11 would immediately find himself in a very tempting situation. He could throw caution to the wind, fly out to the tournament and cruise through the draw, earning himself bucket-loads of ranking points and prize money in the process. Perhaps he'd decide it was worth the risk. No wonder the PSA suspended the tournaments.

Even when we are being escorted by armed guards bristling with automatic weapons, we're still not entirely safe. It sounds perverse but sometimes I feel more at risk when the guards are around, since they draw attention to the fact that we are high-profile athletes. I was perhaps most nervous at the 2003 World Open in Lahore when the then president of Pakistan, Pervez Musharraf, came to spectate. In recent years he'd already survived several assassination attempts on his life. It was flattering to have the president watching our matches but, if I'm honest, I couldn't wait for him and his entourage to leave the premises.

In Muslim countries we'll often get transported from the hotel to the tournament venue in an official minibus with an armed guard sitting at the front. They might as well paint a target on the side of the bus. And how do we know the armed guard is on our side anyway? Who's to say he won't turn round and blow us all away with his Kalashnikov?

During that 2009 tournament in Mumbai I was often tempted to forgo the official transport and, instead, sneak out the back of the hotel, hail a rickshaw and travel to the venue incognito. Weirdly, I felt much more secure.

All the different nationalities travel on those tournament minibuses: players, officials, media, the whole lot. Including all the players from Middle Eastern countries. They get really nervous about the security situation, too, even in their own countries. While I was writing this book, Egyptian player Amr Shabana was in the process of moving his entire family to Canada. The Egyptian national coach Amir Wagih was moving his family – including his highly talented tennis-playing son – to the United States. A lot of the Egyptian players are from well-off, well-educated, liberal families. Some of them attended Western schools in Egypt and are fairly Western in their outlook. They are scared that the fundamentalists want to reshape Egypt into some sort of Iran. As I was writing this, the country was steeped in protests and violence. For that reason it was very difficult for the PSA to sanction any high-profile tournaments there.

To be honest, we players don't really discuss politics that much. It's a bit taboo, always very much the elephant in the room. We don't want to tempt fate or jinx ourselves by discussing fundamentalism. We just want to compete, win matches and get out of dangerous countries intact.

Whenever I'm asked if I am political myself, my immediate response is: "Not in the slightest". I'd much rather follow the latest sports results than current affairs. It's true that, since we travel the world so much, we have a unique insight into all the different cultures we experience. I can't think of many people my age who have travelled the globe as much as I have. Yet I would never pretend to be any sort of expert on world geopolitics.

Despite the travel, we really do live in a bubble. We arrive at the airport, where we are whisked straight to the hotel and then to the tournament venue. If you wanted to, you could spend a whole week competing in a country without ever meeting any locals except to show your passport at immigration and the hotel reception. That sounds terrible, but it's true.

For that reason it would be utterly naive of me to pretend to have informed opinions about international politics. As for international transport, well, that's a different matter. I am a very seasoned expert indeed when it comes to airports, visas, hotels and crossing borders; a rather reluctant expert, I must add.

If you've ever been stuck in an airport, twiddling your thumbs, waiting for a delayed plane, you'll know exactly what I mean. I hate to think of the endless hours I have wasted in airport terminals, cursing various airlines and various ground staff. Welcome to life on the professional squash tour.

Aside from a particularly scary flight back home from Malaysia when we plunged 10,000 feet through an air pocket in a matter of seconds, I think my worst airline nightmare was in 2003 when I reached the quarter-finals of the US Open in Boston. It was a major breakthrough, placing me inside the world top 20 for the first time.

My next stop on the tour was Karachi in Pakistan, requiring a flight via London Heathrow. I hadn't expected to get so far in Boston, so my connection was a bit tight. Yes, you guessed it, all my bags got lost en route. I arrived in Karachi with just my hand luggage and the clothes on my back. It's not the best city to arrive in unprepared – there are no Sports Direct superstores there. Forced to borrow squash clothing and rackets from other competitors, it was hardly the ideal start to the tournament.

That week I got to know the airline rep very well indeed. It wasn't long before we were on first name terms. I was calling him at least twice a day, hoping vainly that my bags might arrive before the tournament started. Every day he'd reassure me in the most optimistic terms that they were on the way.

Day one of the tournament arrived and I was still without any of my bags, so I borrowed a pair of squash shoes from Gregory Gaultier, and some shorts, shirts and rackets from my roommate Peter Barker. The rackets and clothing weren't so bad but the shoes, although they were the right size, weren't a brand I was used to and after just three minutes they had battered and bruised my heels. I ended up losing my first-round match to a completely unknown 15-year-old Pakistani guy called Farhan Mehboob. (As an adult he later reached No.16 in the world.) The week before, I'd been in the quarter-finals of the US Open, and now I was losing to a 15-year-old. It shows you just how important the correct preparation (not to mention equipment) is.

That evening I went to the airport to catch a plane home to the UK. I went up to the airline desk to be greeted by my airline rep friend with a massive grin on his face. "Mr Matthew!" he exclaimed jubilantly. "I have all your bags right here!" I told him to put them straight back on the next plane to London, not even bothering to open them.

Most years I have to endure up to 20 international flights, always economy class. With all that cabin air passing through my lungs – plus the lowered immunity that many top-level sportsmen suffer from – I contract my fair share of bugs and infections. On my return from Pakistan I fell to a dose of glandular fever. I remember sitting at home on the sofa, shivering with fever and watching England win the Rugby World Cup. That last-minute drop goal from Jonny Wilkinson managed to perk me up just a little. Ironically, though, my glandular fever led to one of my luckiest winning streaks ever.

The following week I was due to play in Qatar but with glandular fever coursing through my body I didn't hold up much hope of playing well, especially since I was due to take on Jonathon Power, then world No.3, in the first round. My plan – a fairly cynical one, I admit – was to play Jonathon as best I could, lose the match, take my first-round points and prize money, and head home again to regroup before the World Championships in Pakistan the following week. It was the only time in my career that I'd turned up for a match fully prepared to head straight for the airport once it was over. I even had my bags packed, ready to jump in a taxi.

Ironically, when you have nothing to lose, and no expectations of winning, you often play more freely than if you have your sights set on victory. And so it was with my match against Jonathon. I ended up playing brilliantly against a player who was one of the world's best at that time. It was one game all and I was 10-5 up in the third game when he suddenly pushed away from me and, in one of those inexplicable accidents you sometimes get, he broke a finger in his left hand. At first I thought he was making the whole thing up. There he was, writhing around on the floor in agony, screaming and holding his finger. Jonathon was always prone to a bit of theatrics but this was ridiculous. He looked like an Italian striker who'd dived majestically in the penalty box.

It turned out the injury was completely legitimate. He had indeed broken his finger simply by pushing off from my back. The referee gave him what's called a 'contributed injury'.

In the rules of squash, there are three types of injury. First up is self-inflicted – such as banging your hand against the wall – in which case you have three minutes to recover or you default the match. The second type is contributed – such as players accidentally knocking their heads together – in which case you have an hour to recover and then longer if the tournament schedule permits. The third type is opponent-inflicted – such as being whacked intentionally by your opponent's racket. If it's a serious injury then the match is awarded to the injured player.

When it came to Jonathon's finger, the ref decided both he and I had caused the injury; my back had broken his finger. The match was halted so that he could get treatment, and he obviously required a lot longer than an hour.

The following day Jonathon turned up to the tournament venue with a massive splint on his finger, his arm in a sling. Weeks wouldn't have been long enough for him to recover, so I was awarded a walkover which put me into the second round against the Finnish player Olli Tuominen. Olli and I had played countless times in the juniors and on this occasion I managed to get the better of him. That meant I advanced to meet David Palmer in the quarters. David was carrying an injury, not on his best form. True to the great champion he was, however, he put up a tremendous fight but I managed to squeeze through in four tight games. I eventually lost to Lee Beachill in the semi-finals.

That week I had to change my airline ticket four times. It taught me a valuable lesson: always book to fly home the day after the final, no matter how bad you might be feeling. After losing to Lee I flew straight to Lahore for the World Open and reached the quarter-finals from an unseeded position.

So from entering the tournament with the remnants of glandular fever, fully expecting to lose first round, I then fluked my way through to the semis, shooting up the rankings to No.11 in the world. I'd been languishing between 20 and 30 in the world for a year, my career at a plateau, when all of a sudden I'd got a lucky break. In this sport you never know when a lucky break might come your way, so you just ride the wave when it does. The following year I'd reached No.5 in the world and I've pretty much remained in the world top 10 ever since.

CHAPTER 21

Peeing in front of strangers

In which Nick exposes his genitals to complete strangers and gets offered $18,000 for a car he wins in a tournament.

I could never have one-night stands with random girls. Even if I was a single man (and fancied that sort of thing), it would be impossible. The anti-doping rules in squash mean I have to tell WADA (the World Anti-Doping Agency) where I'm sleeping every single night of the year. Without fail.

This whereabouts rule, as it's known, is designed so that doping controllers can spring surprise tests on us any day they like. I have to tell them exactly where I'll be at a certain hour every day. Whether I'm training, competing abroad, staying with friends or on holiday, I have to let them know. I normally plump for between 7am and 8am since I know I'm either in bed or having breakfast.

WADA try to make it as convenient as possible for us, supplying an email address and phone number so that we can alert them of a change in our whereabouts up to one minute before our allocated testing hour. Still, it's a bit of a pain in the backside, to be frank, but it's the only way the system can be failsafe. Hence the difficulty of one-night stands.

There are actually surprisingly few doping tests in squash. The most I've ever been tested was during the last Commonwealth Games year, 2010, when I had to pee in a sample pot around eight times. Half of those were during tournaments, the other half at my house.

The tournament tests are the easier ones. They normally take place once the match is over. You're allowed to warm down for a few minutes while the tester stays within a few metres of you, keeping an eye on you the whole time.

Then comes the humiliating bit. The tester accompanies you into the toilet cubicle and watches as you produce your sample. He (and for male athletes it always is a he) must actually watch the urine being expelled from your penis so that he knows for sure you're not giving a false sample. In some countries you actually have to take your trousers right down, spin around and prove you haven't got a prosthetic penis stuffed in your trousers. (I think the embarrassment would be worse than the fine.) It's a pretty grim operation all round.

Even grimmer when the tester comes to your house. Although I must say most of them are very affable. Which is why I always offer them a cup of tea. There's this one lady who turns up at my house a few times a year. She always comes with her son because women aren't allowed to watch you pee. So, instead, her teenage son has to squeeze into the toilet cubicle with me and oversee proceedings.

The one bonus is that I never have any problem producing a sample. More often than not the tests take place the morning I get back from a tournament. So there's a good chance my bladder's full since I've either been on a long-haul flight or out on the town, celebrating a win.

I did once miss a test, though. It was when I first started going out with Esme, and I'd decided to stay over at her old place in Manchester. At 7am I got a phone call from my neighbour telling me there was a woman knocking on my front door, so I immediately jumped in the car and headed home. Unfortunately I didn't make it back within the hour, causing a temporary black mark on my testing record. You are only allowed three such no-shows before it constitutes a failed test. I now make sure I update my whereabouts religiously.

Given the obvious inconvenience, occasionally you feel like getting your own back on the testers. I remember one particularly cold and rainy morning in November 2012. I was snuggled up in bed when the doorbell rang insistently. I peeked out through my curtains and immediately recognised who it was. So I let him stand out in the wet for a bit longer. Spiteful, I know, but immensely satisfying.

As we travel round the world on the PSA tour, the quality of doping tests varies enormously. It's sometimes quite astonishing.

There is supposed to be a uniform system, overseen by WADA, identical in whichever country you're competing in. In my experience, this is very rarely the case.

In France we have been allowed to guzzle beer in the testing room while celebrating an England team win. That night there were two testers for the eight players competing in the final and I can assure you those testers didn't check properly as we all produced our samples. In Taiwan I was once asked to produce a second sample because the pH level of my urine was too low. Basically, I'd drunk too much water beforehand. It was late and the tester wanted to go to bed so we didn't bother doing a second test. In the USA, such is the stringency of the testing procedure and the accompanying interrogation that I always feel like some sort of criminal, even though I've never done anything wrong.

The strangest doping story of all happened in Saudi Arabia in 2010 when I won the World Open for the first time. As well as the prize money, there was a tournament prize of a brand new Volkswagen Jetta car. After the semi-final, while I was waiting to give my urine sample, the tester asked me if he could buy the car from me, should I win the whole tournament. He wanted it as a present for his wife and promised to come to my hotel room the morning after the final with $18,000 in cash. I think he might have been taking the piss in more ways than one since he never turned up. In any case, we had to catch an early flight to India.

Most disturbing of all, though, are the rumours I've heard about players from some nations being exempted from testing. Apparently, at one stage, certain Egyptian players were carrying letters stating that they'd already been tested back home in Egypt and that their religion forbade them from being tested abroad since they weren't allowed to show their genitals to a stranger. I don't know if these rumours are true. I'm not sure how I'd feel if they were.

I actually believe there should be more doping tests in squash than there currently are. The sport already has an unbelievably clean record, but we should never get complacent. Some within the sport rightly say that there is no drug in existence that can help you hit the nick and win matches through shot accuracy. But they are missing the point. It's mainly about recovery. If players really wanted to use drugs to enhance their performance on court then they'd be taking substances that aided recovery between matches or helped them train harder.

There are definitely faults in the system. It's only been very recently that we've been required to have blood tests on top of the normal urine tests. Throughout the year prior to writing this book, the testers took random samples of my blood in order to spot any unusual patterns. They call it an 'athlete passport'. Apparently it's easier to spot doping cheats through anomalies in an athlete's blood than by specifically testing for illegal substances. Why was this system not introduced sooner? Is it simply a matter of funding? I know they've been using it in sports such as cycling and skiing for years.

In recent years, I know of two squash players who have been busted for doping – and their drug of choice was cannabis. Now, I know very little about cannabis but I'm pretty sure it won't help your squash. Get stoned and the last thing you'll want to do is play a tough five-game match on a brightly lit squash court.

Nevertheless, both players received bans. I remember one of the situations really clearly. We were competing in the 2011 World Team Championship. A whole load of us got tested after the matches had finished. I was with an Italian team player called Stephane Galifi. He had already received a two-year ban while competing for France six years earlier. And I saw the look on his face when the tester announced that we all had to produce samples. He knew his game was up. Sure enough, it was. He tested positive for "recreational substances" and got slapped with another two-year ban. Silly boy didn't learn his lesson.

I suppose it's good news for squash, however, that there aren't loads of players getting busted for performance-enhancing drugs. Our sport isn't anything like the unholy mess they have in cycling. I'm not condoning the use of recreational drugs, but better we have a tiny bit of cannabis than systematic abuse of human growth hormone.

CHAPTER 22

The pursuit of perfection

In which our man sees the plus side of food poisoning, sprints up and down a swimming pool and learns that there are eight corners in a squash court.

The great Peter Nicol once told me he could think of only five matches throughout his entire career when everything clicked together perfectly. When you consider he was world No.1 for five years and won over 50 tour titles, that shows you just how elusive perfection can be.

As I explained earlier, I can think of only four of my own performances that fall into that category: the final of the Commonwealth Games in Delhi in 2010 when I beat James Willstrop three games to love to win gold; the semi-final of the 2010 World Open in Saudi Arabia when I beat defending champion Amr Shabana in straight games, two of them stretching to tiebreaks; the semi-final of the 2012 Tournament of Champions in New York against Gregory Gaultier where I produced my best short game ever; and, perhaps best of all, the 2012 British Open final when I beat Ramy Ashour three games to love.

Just think. I've been training as a professional player for over 15 years, not to mention all the years of hard graft as a junior. Yet I can think of only four faultless performances during all that time. That blows my mind. Not in a negative way, though. I view it as a massive positive. If perfection wasn't so difficult to find, loads of players would have become world champion. Being successful is so much more rewarding when you remember the countless hours of toil that got you there – the blood, sweat and tears that are spilt on the court, in the gym, and behind the scenes. The whole thing really is a cumulative effort. I don't think I've ever met a world-class sportsman or woman who has achieved anything by cutting corners or by taking the easy path. The downs always outnumber the ups. That's why the feeling of elation is so gratifying.

After a big win my first thoughts are often about the gruelling physical sessions I might have done with Mark Campbell or the technical adjustments I've perhaps worked on with DP. In the bright light of victory, these sessions might seem relatively insignificant but it is this hard graft behind the scenes that ultimately makes the difference between success and failure.

**

Commonwealth Games singles final
Delhi, India, October 2010
Beat James Willstrop 11-6, 11-7, 11-7 (66 minutes)

In the run-up to the Commonwealth Games final against James Willstrop in 2010, I was the favourite: No.1 in the world and No.1 seed in the tournament. In the comfort of the athletes' village, on the TV, I'd watched with relish as James was forced into a brutal late-night quarter-final against David Palmer. While James was carrying out his statutory doping test at two o'clock in the morning, I was tucked up in bed, getting a restful night's sleep. We both then had semi-finals to negotiate, which we both won in straight games, but the after-effects of that Palmer match must still have been taking its toll on James's body when it came to the final two days later.

However, when you're the favourite, it's crucial you never think of yourself as such. Even the tiniest bit of complacency can make the difference between a good start to a match and a bad start. The last thing you need is to be on the back foot at the start. At the time I was also enjoying a long winning streak against James, stretching all the way back to December 2007. As I mentioned earlier in the book, despite this streak, I never once allowed myself to feel even remotely complacent against James. He is far too good a player for this. Add to that his determination and his legendary ability to dig himself out of seemingly impossible positions.

Strangely, I think the food poisoning I'd been suffering from in the weeks before the Commonwealth Games might have been a blessing in disguise. In the early rounds I knew I was some way below my best. But I never got frustrated or set my expectations too high. Given my illness, I was just delighted to be there. The Commonwealth gold medal was something I'd had my sights set on for the previous four years, ever since I witnessed Peter Nicol's inspiring win in Melbourne in 2006. With squash yet to be an Olympic sport, the Commonwealth Games takes on extra significance. It's always seen by a much wider audience than any other squash event and it's the only tournament properly followed by mainstream sports fans. With this in mind, I felt there was a risk I might hype up the event too much for my own good. The food poisoning forced me to focus on just one match at a time.

In the final I got my nose in front, right at the start, and then stayed that way until the very end. The only time I fell behind in the score was in the third game, and by that stage I was already two games up. On match ball I remember James playing a forehand boast from the back of the court which sat up perfectly on my backhand side. Normally in a situation like that I'd have about 15 different shot options cluttering my mind but on this occasion I was crystal clear. I caught the backhand drop shot (DP's favourite shot, by the way) so perfectly that it rolled out of the nick between the side wall and the floor. For once I had executed it like the master technician DP. My racket fell on the floor, my arms went up in the air and I had this gormless yet ecstatic look on my face – the look I often have when I'm trying to grasp the significance of what I've just achieved. There I was, standing on that podium with the song Jerusalem bringing me to tears as the St. George's cross was raised high above the stands. It was of course an incredibly proud moment. To produce such a performance in such a big match, and to do it with my mum, dad and Auntie Sue in the audience, made it even prouder.

***

World Open semi-final
Al Khobar, Saudi Arabia, December 2010
Beat Amr Shabana 11-6, 12-10, 12-10 (59 minutes)

Going back on the PSA tour after winning the Commonwealth
Games was a strange feeling – almost an anti-climax. The 2010
Games had fallen mid-season so tournaments continued the very
next week. I decided to sit out an Egyptian event in El Gouna and
then, after that, I lost early to Daryl Selby in Kuwait. I was two
games up and suddenly I hit a brick wall. Mentally I was shot. After
such a big win I was finding it incredibly difficult to push myself
psychologically. The fact that the World Open in Saudi Arabia was
less than a month away was very worrying indeed.

Then the weather turned against me. The day I was due to fly
out to Saudi there was loads of snow on the road. We got stuck in
horrendous traffic en route to Manchester Airport. It was the first
time in my career that I ever missed a flight.

At the World Open there's always the PSA annual general
meeting the night before the first round. Arriving a day late, I
missed this meeting. All the other players were talking about the
issues raised and I felt very much left out. But, just like the food
poisoning before the Commonwealth Games, this somehow took
the pressure off me. There was the added benefit of extra rest days
during the tournament which really helped. That year the Worlds
were spread over 10 days meaning that, should you make it to the
final, you'd have three or four rest days en route. It felt more like
a tennis Grand Slam than a regular squash tournament where we
usually compete every day.

By the time I reached the semi-final – up against Amr Shabana
– I was confident. Amr was the reigning world champion for the
fourth time and the general consensus amongst the other players
was that, if he was up for it, he was the best player in the world. The
big question was: "Was he really up for it?"

The minute I started that semi-final match I discovered he
most certainly was. He badly wanted that fifth World Open title.

I started strongly, winning the first game 11-6, but then got put through the ringer for the following two games. Amr's length on his forehand is the best in the sport. Couple that with his forehand volley and you face a lethal combination. The fact he is a left-hander and attacks the backhand of most of his right-handed opponents makes this combination unplayable at times. During that match I was bombarded with a torrent of Shabana forehand drives and volleys, but somehow survived. It was thanks to all the work DP and I had done reconstructing my backhand all those years ago. Every time Amr forged a lead, I would claw my way back level. He was outplaying me yet the scores remained even.

That week in Saudi, on my rest days, DP and I spent most of our time working on a surprise tactic: the trickle boast. (Just a quick explanation for any reader not fully versed in squash technique: a boast is a shot that hits the side wall before reaching the front wall. A trickle boast is a boast shot played right up at the front of the court that trickles round the corners and stays as low as possible to the floor.) DP thought that against the Egyptians my attritional style of play would frustrate them only up to a certain point. After a while I would become too predictable. Therefore I needed more counter-attacking weapons in my armoury – hence the trickle boast. Against Amr I was under the cosh but I battled my way to match point at 11-10. Frankly, had the match gone to a fourth game, I didn't fancy my chances. So I shaped up for a big forehand and, at the last second, rolled my wrist over for a trickle boast. Amr went the wrong way and duly snapped his racket over his knee in frustration. I was in the final and it was all thanks to DP's cheeky little trickle boast.

The next day, in the final, I beat James Willstrop to become world champion for the first time. A lot was made in the press about James having had a tougher run than me, spending longer on court in earlier rounds. Supposedly he was more fatigued than me in the final. I, however, feel that if you can beat Amr Shabana 3-0 – something of a rare occurrence – then you fully deserve any extra freshness you might have.

***

Tournament of Champions semi-final
New York City, USA, January 2012
Beat Gregory Gaultier 11-8, 11-9, 9-11, 11-4 (75 minutes)

New York 2012. I'd just spent the month of December and the entire Christmas period sitting on the sofa, watching James Willstrop rise to the top of the world rankings. I had a tear at the top of my right hamstring. During this period, the only exercise I could do was very light rehabilitation exercises in the gym, treading water in the swimming pool and technical work on court. I couldn't place any serious weight on my right leg but DP and I managed to get on court most days for static practices.

As I explained before, having time out from the hectic life on tour can sometimes be a blessing in disguise since it allows you to work on things you otherwise wouldn't consider. Because I couldn't put enough weight through my right leg to hit the ball hard, we instead concentrated on my touch game at the front of the court. It became a challenge for me to see how softly I could hit my drop shots, and how close to the front wall I could get the ball to bounce twice. As well as honing an area of my game which wasn't that strong, DP was also keeping me sane during my injury lay-off.

The sessions I was doing in the pool, meanwhile, maintained my fitness. My physio, Jade, would bark at me like a sergeant-major while I put on a flotation belt and did brutally intense high-knee sprints up and down the pool. In January, with the Tournament of Champions looming, my injury was finally healed, my fitness was good and I had a serious point to prove: I had just lost my world No.1 ranking to James and I badly wanted it back. My new short game was also ready to be tried out.

It worked to brilliant effect. In the semi-final against Gregory Gaultier, one of the fastest players on tour, I managed to hit more winners with drop shots and volley drops in a single match than I usually would in an entire tournament. DP had struck gold again. I went on to beat James in the final and take my first Tournament of Champions title. For a short time I regained the world No.1 ranking.

***

British Open final
London, UK, May 2012
Beat Ramy Ashour 11-9, 11-4, 11-8 (49 minutes)

My 2012 British Open win over Ramy Ashour, at London's O2 Arena, is, I believe, the finest performance of my entire career. As I admitted earlier in the book, I'd previously become obsessed with Ramy after a succession of losses to him during 2011 and 2012. I'd heard stories of how Peter Nicol had once adapted his training specifically to beat Jansher Khan, and I'd tried to do the same for Ramy. The key difference, and where I got it wrong, was that Peter looked at how he might hurt Jansher. I, on the other hand, focused on what Ramy was good at and how I might stop him, instead of concentrating on my own strengths. This was approaching the problem the wrong way round.

In the build-up to the 2012 British Open I worked with my sports psychologist Mark Bawden, who encouraged me to focus on my own strengths. He got me thinking about how I could hurt Ramy rather than how Ramy could hurt me. I needed good length on my shots, and I needed to hit extra-wide cross-court shots because Ramy was so strong in the middle of the court. But these strategies alone were not enough. They would limit Ramy but not defeat him. I still needed to dominate the middle of the court by pushing him deep and controlling with my volleys. Then I needed to attack with more variety and deception than I usually did.

DP had just returned from a trip to Brazil with Chris Gordon, an American player he coaches. Over in South America they'd become friendly with an eccentric Brazilian player called Rafael Alarcon. Over dinner one night, Rafa said to DP that when I played Ramy I "didn't play enough to the eight corners of the court". DP had no idea what he was talking about. Eight corners? Surely, even in Brazil, there are only four corners to a squash court.

Rafa explained that he considered the areas on both side walls, just in front of and just behind the service box, to be corners of the court. Eight corners in all. If I were to use these extra corners, it would slow Ramy's speed to the front of the court and limit his counterattack because of a lack of angles. Most crucially, though, it would give me more variation in my attack.

The O2 Arena was a fantastic venue. I loved the feeling of playing in it. But even by the time I'd reached the final I still hadn't hit full stride. I was lucky to overcome a slightly tired Peter Barker in the semi-final the day before. Perhaps I was saving my best for last.

In the final itself, Rafa's eight-corner plan dovetailed perfectly with my new mental strategy. Not only did I frustrate the Egyptian into making a succession of errors, but I also managed to attack him too. It was my third British Open title, more than any other Englishman had won. After the match I was annoyed to read some reports that suggested I won through Ramy's errors rather than my own good play. I felt I had executed a perfect plan that day and deserved more credit. The fact that, at the time of writing, I haven't beaten Ramy since shows just how elusive perfection can be.

***

There's one thing I believe these four matches have in common: clarity. Each time I managed to play at my highest level, I had a clear game plan and the feeling that I had total control in how to execute it. My thought processes were clear. When you're thinking clearly and you have a mind uncluttered by extraneous thoughts, the effects are staggering. I have a tendency to over-complicate matters but when I'm playing well, squash can become such a simple game. Positive things then happen naturally. It also helps if I remind myself of that famous acronym KISS: Keep It Simple Stupid.

***

At the start of this chapter I told you how Peter Nicol had five matches where everything clicked together perfectly. Where's my fifth match then? I'm hoping it's still to come.

CHAPTER 23

Faster, higher, stronger

In which Nick considers a second career after squash, tries
to persuade his wife to hold off on babies and contemplates
Tiger Woods with his trousers down.

London 2012. Olympic Games men's singles final. One game all,
10-all in the decider. I can feel the tension. I have been involved
in close matches many times before but never quite like this. More
than 6,000 people are packed into London's Wembley Arena. The
noise is electrifying, and not surprisingly considering the biggest
title in the sport is at stake: an Olympic gold medal.

I'm a nervous wreck. The player on the other side of the court
shows no emotion – he looks in complete control. A left-hander, he
has great speed and power, and certainly isn't short of grace. He is
the most deceptive player in the sport and has this unnerving ability
to wrong-foot opponents almost at will. Four-times world champion
and considered by many the greatest player of all time, he knows
full well how to close these sorts of matches out. There don't seem
to be any chinks at all in his armour. The pace at which he plays
is relentless. His court coverage has been phenomenal. The speed
at which he unleashes his forehand is extraordinary. No opponent
could normally withstand such a barrage for this long. Something
has to give sooner or later.

But his opponent isn't budging. He has a magnificent defence
and isn't short of a bit of attacking flair himself. A counter-puncher,
he's a master at turning defence into attack. Standing far up in
the middle of the court, he looks to intercept every shot as early as
possible. His lobs disappear high into the roof before coming back
down to earth with amazing accuracy. He is stubbornly tough and

plays every point as if it's his last. His opponent is forced to bust a gut for every single point. This player reminds me a bit of myself.

I am high up in the stands watching this drama unfold from a distance. It isn't me on the court, but Lee Chong Wei, the Malaysian former world No.1 badminton player. The left-hander in question is Chinese badminton player Lin Dan, but blink and it could just as well be squash player Amr Shabana. They are remarkably similar, not just as left-handers and in the style of play they employ, but also with the number of world titles they have won.

This may be badminton rather than squash but many of the actions are the same. The lunges are deep, the footwork fast, the reactions rapid. Badminton is the Olympic sport which most resembles squash. That explains why I was so desperate for tickets to this event. I wanted to imagine what it might have been like if squash had been featured at the London Olympics. What would it have felt like had I myself been able to step out for an Olympic final? In summer 2012 I would have been at the peak of my game. But with squash failing to gain Olympic status for either 2016 or 2020, any faint chance I may have had of competing in an Olympic Games has now disappeared.

I'm certainly not planning on retiring any time soon but I have to admit I'm no longer a spring chicken. In squash, when you hit your mid-30s, you start to slow down a little. As I write this, I am enjoying my 33rd summer.

I'm still up among the world's top four players but I've been catching myself doing a bit of soul searching recently. 2010 and 2011 were undoubtedly my best years while, in 2013, my form dropped a bit. Am I on a downward slope? Can I still improve? Most importantly, do I still have the hunger to strive for more? I once read a quote from the legendary distance runner, Haile Gebrselassie, which for me perfectly sums up retirement from sport. He said the minute you start to think about retirement, you are already retired. That's why I'm trying my best not to think about it.

How long my squash career lasts is in some ways out of my control. I have no way of planning exactly when I might retire – injury or a lack of form could dictate that for me. But I really want to enjoy my twilight years in my sport. I've already achieved more than I ever dreamed of. What's important is that I play free of fear, with a smile on my face, and with no self-imposed pressure to perform.

Retirement from sport is a strange old thing. For most of us, the pipe and slippers come out when we're still 30-somethings, forcing us to consider a second career that could last another 30 years or so. In the more sedentary sports, on the other hand, like golf, snooker or darts, there's nothing to stop you competing at a high level when you're close to receiving your free bus pass.

It always makes sense to retire on a high, while you're still winning matches. Having reached No.1 in the world, it would be ridiculous for me to soldier on into my 40s, gradually sliding down the rankings and losing to players half my age. Forgive me if it sounds vain, but I can't imagine anything more humiliating.

Not that I haven't got plenty of fuel left in my tank. Jonah Barrington, arguably the greatest British player ever to set foot on a squash court, was still running with the big boys at the age of 40. As my dad reminded me on my 33rd birthday, Hashim Khan didn't win his first British Open until he was 35. He then went on to win six more.

If athletes do decide to bow out gracefully, it's always timely if they coincide their final tournament with a major event. Next year's Commonwealth Games in Glasgow, for example, could be a great swansong, although I'd hope to last well beyond that. The Commonwealth Games after that are in the Australian city Gold Coast in 2018. What an amazing venue that promises to be. If squash ever qualifies for the Olympics, that would be the best curtain call any professional player could ask for.

One day squash will eventually join the Olympic family. There's a chance I'll be long retired by then, however. It may not even be during my lifetime. But mark my words, one day it will be an Olympic sport.

It's a real injustice that it hasn't yet been included. For a long time squash has ticked all the boxes when it comes to the Olympic motto of faster, higher, stronger (citius, altius, fortius). There are loads of existing Olympic sports where none of these elements apply – rhythmic gymnastics, for example, or synchronised swimming or diving. Granted, the artistic aspects of these events are amazing (I couldn't do that kind of thing in a million years), but how on earth do you really tell who's won? So much of it is down to the aesthetic taste of the judges.

Squash is a truly global sport, played in over 180 countries around the world. It's a combative one-on-one gladiatorial fight. There are successful men's and women's professional tours. There have been world champions from all six continents. It's a popular sport across the Muslim world. It's a great sport for kids. You can easily erect temporary courts pretty much anywhere you want, making venues cheap to build. If it was an Olympic sport you could use the courts brilliantly to showcase iconic areas of the host city.

Of course, I'm bound to say all this. I'm biased.

So why haven't bids yet been successful? Let's face it: squash needs a really big kick up the arse. We should have joined the Olympics in the 1980s – the golden age when squash was even more popular around the world than it currently is. By the 1990s and 2000s that popularity had waned somewhat. It wasn't until 2005 (the start of the bidding process for the 2012 Olympics) that we submitted our first really serious bid.

For 2012, the International Olympic Committee was keen to sign up both squash and karate. But then, at the last minute, there were budgetary problems which meant they couldn't afford to add more sports. As squash's bid reached its climax, we England players were all training in Manchester as a national squad and watching closely while events unfolded on TV. Everyone thought we were in. It was the biggest kick in the guts when we missed out, especially with our capital city winning the rights to host the Games. I was at the peak of my powers in 2012 and I would have had a real shot at winning gold.

By the time the 2016 bid came around it was all about commercialism. The IOC realised that a high-profile sport like golf would attract more viewers than squash. And they've got a point. Millions more people will watch Tiger Woods hitting one 400-yard drive off the tee than all of the archery or weightlifting events for the entire Olympic Games. (Fortunately – for golf – the IOC voted to include golf just a few days before Woods got caught with his trousers down. It would have been interesting to see if the sport's bid had been successful had the vote taken place a couple of weeks later.) With squash missing out on 2016, my last realistic chance for an Olympic medal was gone.

While watching the Olympics in London I found it fascinating to see sports I wouldn't usually follow. I wasn't interested in the tennis or the football, and I'm sure I won't be interested in golf in 2016. But alongside the cycling and the athletics (I was in the Olympic stadium on Super Saturday when Great Britain won three track and field golds), I loved watching the handball, the rowing, the water polo and the volleyball – all sports that rarely find themselves in the limelight. I think lesser-known sports are what the Olympics are really all about. It gives them their 15 minutes of fame once every four years. Squash should have shared with that in London. We also missed out on the chance to inspire youngsters and encourage them to try out squash for the first time.

In the old days everyone used to moan that squash didn't work on TV. And they had a point. But nowadays, thanks to technological advances and a few bright ideas, it makes for a superb TV sport. We have all-glass courts so that live spectators and TV viewers can watch from every angle. Video replays have been introduced, allowing referees to adjudicate with confidence, and cutting down on laborious arguments over strokes and lets. Arena music (like in boxing) and player nicknames (like in darts and snooker) lend more excitement to the lead-ups to the matches. The height of the tin has been lowered to encourage more attacking play. Even the scoring system has been changed to create more exciting critical points. But the greatest benefit of all for TV viewers has been the introduction of high-definition TV. It's now so much easier to track the ball while watching the TV screen.

Squash TV has already done wonders for our sport. Yet we need more matches featured on mainstream TV platforms. It's great that the 2013 World Championships in Manchester were covered by the BBC but, apart from the Commonwealth Games, when was the last time you saw a squash match on terrestrial TV? I heard that a few years ago the PSA actually offered TV rights to the BBC for free, but the corporation wasn't able to accept them because squash didn't have Olympic status.

When tournaments are staged in iconic locations such as the Great Pyramids in Egypt, or New York's Grand Central Terminal, this encourages TV producers to get involved. Perhaps we should aim for even more exciting locations. It's not difficult to arrange.

Squash courts are relatively small compared to other fields of play, and it's easy to construct temporary courts. Imagine how cool it would be if the world's top players were all competing in front of the Taj Mahal or in Times Square, or beneath the Eiffel Tower, or next to the Leaning Tower of Pisa, or outside the Sydney Opera House. A squash court in Trafalgar Square might have been the iconic image of London 2012. The other benefit of competing near a famous city attraction is that thousands of passers-by get to see the sport in action. Just look at the publicity we get at the Tournament of Champions in New York City. Millions of commuters pass through Grand Central Terminal every week. Even if they get just a ten-second glimpse of squash, that might be enough to spark an interest.

***

I may have a family soon, which will surely change my perspective on squash and life in general. My wife, Esme, is certainly very keen to have babies soon. I'm keen, too, although I'd be happy to wait a little longer before I hear the pitter patter of little feet.

Outside of professional competition I have a few irons in a few fires. One of my greatest passions right now is the Nick Matthew Squash Academy which I set up at Hallamshire and Abbeydale clubs in 2012. I'm hoping it will grow exponentially over the years, offering junior and adult coaching alike. My ultimate aim is to create a breeding ground for budding young professionals where they can learn all about technique, tactics, fitness, even the business side of the sport. Hopefully, along with the national governing body, England Squash & Racketball, we can help produce a champion of the future; one to rival the Egyptians who are threatening to utterly dominate the game. At junior level they are currently winning everything. Things have become so bad that English kids now hold Egyptian players too much in awe. Many English kids look like they've already lost before they even step on court. I often hear them saying: "I'm playing an Egyptian next, so he/she must be strong". I'd love to help change this mentality and make English juniors the best in the world; make them the feared rather than the fearful players.

I'd also love to expand my academy so that it links with British school sport. The ultimate dream is to start a charitable squash school which, alongside academic education, introduces the sport to youngsters from deprived communities. There are many successful examples of this in the United States: SquashBusters in Boston, for example, and StreetSquash in New York. I've always been inspired by these charities and by meeting the kids involved.

Perhaps I could take the academy around the country, even around the world, using roadshows, clinics and exhibition matches. I love visiting those classic, old-school squash clubs where you find the real die-hard players and fans. They are the people who have the deepest passion for the game.

There are other great job opportunities within the sport. Thanks to Squash TV, there might be a few vacancies for squash commentators in the future. If you've ever met me, you'll know the Yorkshireman in me never struggles for an opinion on anything. With me on the microphone, there would never be any risk of dead air. I certainly wouldn't be short of things to say and would hopefully provide a valuable insight on the battles you get in professional squash.

I feel honoured to have been on the PSA tour for the last 15 years. What has been especially precious to me is that I feel I've spanned three distinct generations of players. In my younger days I was lucky to be up against the likes of Peter Nicol and Jonathon Power. They were idols for me when I was growing and yet I managed to draw level with them towards the end of their careers. One of my best wins ever was when I beat Jonathon 3-2 at the Tournament of Champions in New York in 2006 while he was No.1 in the world. He retired the very next day. I hope it wasn't the shame of losing to me that finally tipped him over the edge. He recently revealed to me that I am the player he encourages his juniors to emulate the most. That's a massive compliment for me. And to think I never used to believe he rated me as a player.

When Power and Nicol retired it opened the doors for a whole new generation of players led by James Willstrop, Amr Shabana, Gregory Gaultier, Ramy Ashour and me. Some of my most memorable moments on tour have been the humdinger matches I've had with these guys: those matches where everything is left on the court afterwards. I've been lucky to have had at least one such match with each of the main rivals of my generation: Ramy in Saudi Arabia in 2009, James at Canary Wharf in 2010, Amr in New York in 2011 and Greg at the World Teams in 2013. In the previous chapter I pointed out how hard it is to reach perfection individually on court. For two players to do it at the same time and on the same day is incredibly rare. The matches were on big stages, too. I'm sure, in years to come, we will reminisce much more about these matches than any of the titles we might have won.

My peers and I (Ramy excepted) are all well towards the latter stages of our careers now, and there's a crop of younger players snapping at our heels, just as keen, just as determined as we once were. Newer players like Mohamed El Shorbagy, Omar Mosaad and Tarek Momen all compete with such confidence, never displaying an ounce of fear. They go for broke, every match they play. (Mental note to self: retire before these youngsters start to make me feel old and sluggish.)

How things have changed in this sport while I've been competing. When I first started out we scored to nine points, we played with a 19-inch tin and most of the courts were made of concrete. Nowadays it's scoring to 11, a 17-inch tin and all-glass courts pretty much across the board. Squash TV now follows every shot we hit. The prize money has improved drastically. When I first started competing, a $50,000 event was so rare that most of the world top 10 would enter it. Nowadays there are so many lucrative tournaments being staged that a $50,000 event might attract only two or three players from the top 10. We're certainly not rewarded in the same way as professional tennis players or golfers, but it's an improvement nonetheless.

The style of play has changed radically, too, partly due to lighter rackets. Most players, led by the new breed of Egyptians, use their wrists much more than in the previous generation, moving the ball faster around the court. Back in the old days squash was a deeply attritional game with players grinding out long rallies. Today's players favour more of an all-court game. Look at Tarek Momen, Saurav Ghosal and Miguel Angel Rodriguez, for example. They seem to cover the court like bees swarming over honey —some of the fastest movers I've ever had to face. Often they make me feel like an old man out there on the court. Hopefully I can use the experience I've garnered from 15 years on tour to hold them off for a while longer.

Sometimes I think back to that young Nick Matthew at the Wembley Conference Centre, watching the likes of Jahangir and Jansher Khan do battle in the British Open. It feels so strange to me that there might be kids similarly inspired by watching me play. I would dearly love to inspire them for many more years to come.

ACKNOWLEDGEMENTS

I want to thank my mum and dad for introducing me to this wonderful sport and for giving me the opportunity to have the experiences necessary to write a book about it. I have thoroughly enjoyed reminiscing about my life with you both. Thanks for all your love and support, both on and off the court. I will be always grateful.

Thank you to Esme for being my wife and putting me ahead of everything else. Thank you for being my sounding board and for tolerating me when my head was stuck in the laptop for nights on end.

And to my Auntie Sue for being an inspiration. Your brutal honesty was needed at times, too.

And to Paul Walters for your patience and drive in seeing this project through. Thank you for helping me realise one of my ambitions.

And to Rachel Pullan for all of your hard work behind the scenes. You are the oil that makes the cogs turn.

And to Dominic Bliss for listening to my ramblings and helping me to put them into words. Most of all for your wicked sense of humour which made the book fun at all times.

And to Howard Harding for all of your squash facts and figures. You truly are an encyclopedia of squash.

And to Steve Cubbins, Steve Line, Framboise Gommendy, David Barry, Jordan Mansfield and Luke Gauci for allowing me use of your fantastic images. Also to Keith Dockar for his fantastic wedding photos.

And finally to all of the people I have met on my travels in squash. Thank you for giving me so many fantastic stories to write about. I hope you enjoy reading them.

***

Dominic Bliss is a journalist, editor and author. He has contributed to nearly all the UK national newspapers and many different magazines, and has written eight books.